KISS THE BEAR!
Book II (Revised version)
By Rick Barker

D1555536

Table of Contents

Cover Artwork by Elisha Schaff
Cover Photo by Melonie Eva

To my wife, Marci, and my children, Dustin and
Denai, who have enriched my life beyond my
imagination.
I am thankful to God for Marci, who encourages me
along life's journey, who still laughs at my jokes,
(mostly) and who sticks with me through all of life's
challenges. I thank God for Dustin and Denai, who
have provided me with so many stories and
illustrations over the years!

I thank God for my brother and sisters, Arlene,
Karen, Gale, Rod, and my mom and dad, Lloyd and
Evelyn Barker. I love my family.

 I am also grateful to God for all the people at
Cariboo Christian Life Fellowship, (CCLF) upon
whom I get to bestow my humor, my 'wisdom'--
my style of preaching and leadership—and to know
you still like me…wow… thank you for your love
and patience!

Chapter 1
The Revelation

The Son of Man came to seek and save that which was lost. —Jesus of Nazareth, Luke 19: 10

So, there I was, a 'noble and respected' pastor of a small community in the Interior of British Columbia, about to enter the twilight zone of a local pub—about to go where "no man has gone before" to do what I was about to do. With one more breath of prayer, I pushed open the saloon-style doors and stepped into the foreign world of dimly lit, smoke-filled noise. I squinted to adjust my eyes to my surroundings; heads turned to see who it was that entered their domain, friend or foe, and little did I know that my world was about to be changed forever.

What in the world was I doing, you ask? Well, let me take you back a couple of months prior to venturing out into the neighborhood tavern. Life for me was generally the same as for most pastors—meeting with people, assisting them in their day to day stuff, shepherding them through the speed-bumps and potholes of life, preaching and preparing, praying and leading the family of God, looking at times to that distant question of "How will I reach this community for Christ?" but always coming up a bit short because of all the things that typically fill up a pastor's most precious book besides his Bible—his coveted day-timer. Then one night, God spoke to me in a dream. Now, God has spoken to me many times through dreams, downloading revelation, new ideas, scripture and direction. In fact, my whole step into a life of "full-time" ministry was initiated by the Lord through a dream. My wife, Marci, had told me that very night that she felt God would speak to me in a dream, but as a typical husband, I thought… "Well, whatever…" But He did, and it launched us into ministry, and into an adventuresome journey that I wouldn't trade away for a million bucks. And, while I know some people have trouble with the whole dream thing, I have searched the scriptures and found that there is a huge amount of biblical precedent for God speaking in dreams, both in the Old and the New Testament. Immediately I think of Joseph and his dreams found in Genesis 37; I think of David writing in Psalm 127 how the Lord "gives to His beloved in their sleep," how Daniel called God, "the Giver of dreams and the Interpreter of dreams" (Daniel 5:12), how Daniel himself had dreamt many dreams that stirred his heart.

I think of how Joel prophesied (2:28) that old men will dream dreams, and young men see visions in the last days, and how many dreams played a part in the birth of our Lord Jesus—with Joseph, both in the birth, marriage to Mary, and with the escape to Egypt, and subsequent return to Israel, plus with the Magi, or wise men as well, warning them not to return to Herod but to go home instead by another route. In addition, Peter had dreams from God, and experienced night and day visions, as did John and Paul (the man from Macedonia, plus the Lord speaking to him in Corinth). The list goes on. Anyway, all that to say, I believe we serve the God who speaks today, as Job 33:14 affirms: "God does speak, now one way, now another, though men may not perceive it." Back to the story at hand—God spoke to me in a dream. I dreamt that I was walking along a forest road with my earthly father, who went to be with the Lord in 1989 (my dad was set free from alcoholism dramatically by God and was always quick to tell the story after that). In my dream, I turned to my right and was surprised to see a young boy of around 12 years old with long brown hair out in the wilderness. There was a deep gully on the side of the road where I stood, and a river below; the boy was on the other side of the river walking out from a thicket, leading a donkey that was pulling a cart. He was walking right toward the river and I was afraid for him, although he showed no signs of being uncomfortable. I lost sight of him so I went closer to the edge of the road, to the beginning of the gully to look over to see if I could spot him. There he was walking right into the river! And, I was surprised to see the donkey already in the river—doing the backstroke! It was like a cartoon, as only a donkey could do a backstroke, but I didn't laugh in my dream; it seemed to be no big deal to me at the time. But I was worried about the boy. I turned around to talk to my father and suddenly this boy was in my face. I mean, literally, he was about 12 inches away from my face, now a little larger than a boy and he was peering into my eyes with intensity that blazed like fire. I realized as I looked into his eyes that this was no ordinary boy. It was in fact, Jesus, my Lord, and my Savior and He was looking intently into my very being. He spoke and the sound of the voice was all that I could hear or focus on. These are the words He said: "People look for me in many different ways. But I search for people... in bars, and at parties." Then, not taking His eyes from mine, He gave a coy, almost mischievous smile as if He was about to surprise me, and surprise me He did! He jumped right into me! I mean, He literally leapt into my very chest, inside of my spirit and I awoke from the dream with a start. I sat there awake in the middle of the night, wondering what this meant, and I questioned the Lord on it before falling asleep again. The next morning, my wife Marci and I were heading out of town for a conference and we were discussing the dream. I told her I felt that it was a commission from God. In the dream, Jesus told me He searches for people—that is He's active, not passive. He is searching. His heart really is for the lost, as Matthew 19: 10 declares, "The Son of Man came to seek and save that which was lost."

The donkey and the cart represented the harvest that is ripe. Jesus being represented as a boy seemed to emphasize childlike faith and joy in the harvest. My earthly father being there reinforced evangelism. Jesus is searching, searching... and then He jumps right inside of me. Jesus inside of me, the Hope of Glory, is searching and using my eyes, my hands, my feet, actively looking for the lost and then reaping the harvest. Where? In bars and in parties. Oh, my goodness! Does that mean… do I have to… yes! That was what that coy smile was all about.

This would mean I would have to climb out of my comfort zone and go where the Holy Spirit wanted to go, speak to whom He wanted me to speak, go into the local bar for a starter, and see what He had in mind. The timing had to be right, the prayer-cover, the motivation—everything had to revolve around being obedient to the voice of the Holy Spirit saying "Now, now is the time." As my dad used to say: "When I say jump, you say 'how high?'" So, there I was. It was a Friday night; I was on a prayer walk—believe me I was praying! "Lord, You said You search for people; You are inside of me by Your Holy Spirit. You are directing me to go into the bar tonight; I am simply following Your lead. I have no idea what will take place. Lead on, Lord Jesus."

I pushed opened the doors.

Going deeper…

1) Have you ever had God speak to you in a dream?
2) Has God ever prompted you to do something you would not ordinarily do?
3) How did that turn out?

4) If Jesus came to seek and save that which is lost, what are we doing about that in our day to day life?

5) How is Jesus searching for people through you – through your eyes? Your hands? Your feet?

6) What can you do on your own, or with others, to keep aware of the search mission Jesus has you on today?

Chapter 2
The Harvest

"Look up for the harvest is plentiful but the workers are few. Ask the Lord of the harvest therefore to send out workers into His harvest field." ~ Jesus of Nazareth, (Matthew 9:37)

Now, I must admit I am a fairly well known person in our small town of maybe 2,500 people, partly because I used to be a journalist at the local paper for several years, partly because I am a public entertainer doing ventriloquism now and then, and now there's the pastor thing, which means occasionally leading public funeral services and marriages. And, did I mention that I've lived here for over 40 years? Needless to say, people did double-takes as I walked into that dark cavern of fellowship.

Immediately, I was hit by the smell of beer, which brought flooding back a rash of memories of my own dip into alcohol and drug abuse in my young adult years, but those memories were quickly pushed to the side when I scanned the room and noted about nine backslidden Christians in there. My heart went out to those prodigals, as I am sure the Lord's does as well.

I walked over toward "the bar" of the bar, trying to look as if I knew what I was doing—you know, kind of John Wayne-like. I imagined that this must be what it's like for someone brand new going into a foreign place like a church. "Who do I look at? What do I do? Who do I smile at? Am I supposed to kneel? What is this? A bulletin... oh, am I supposed to do something with it?"

The waitress, a backslidden Christian herself, came up to me with a smile. She knew me and asked boldly, "What are you doing here?" I smiled.

It was one of those times when just the right line was there on the tip of my tongue. "I heard the fishin' was good."

She laughed and asked what I wanted to drink. I shouted at her (you must shout to be heard). "Coke!" and she ambled away. She quickly came back and told me it was on the house. That was nice, I thought.

Well with Coke in hand, I slowly turned around and faced the crowd. I felt like it was slow motion as I was scanning the audience, thinking, praying, "Who are you searching for, Lord?"

My eyes locked with a young man whom I had met just the day before at the local high school. He was a journalist, actually doing the very same job that I used to do a number of years ago. His name was David and he motioned for me to come and sit. He looked like a lost puppy, all by himself in the midst of a crowd. He was in his twenties, had long curly hair and a nice disposition. He was alone so I thought, "Here goes" and I plunged in.

Parenthetically, I should note that when you are in this mode of evangelism, you kind of get into a zone where you simply are doing things, saying things that sometimes even surprise yourself, but if you abide in that place, fixed on the Lord, good things happen. As I said, he indicated for me to sit down, which helped my comfort zone a little.

Others, who knew me, walked by and said things similar to what the waitress had said such as "what are you doing here?" I looked at David. He looked at me. And, then he said this... and remember the context of why I am here, what I am doing, first time to the bar in probably 22 years. Get this... he says, "Man, sometimes I do not know why the @#%& I am here!"

My response came out quicker than I expected it. "I know why!" I shouted back at him.

He looked at me with a quizzical look. I reintroduced myself and then, looking around the room, yelled over the crowd "My father used to live here in this bar! He was the town drunk, until something happened that really changed his life!"

There it goes. That was the casting of the line, or the tossing of the net. Remember Jesus talking about the kingdom of heaven being like a net that is tossed into the lake and becomes full of fish of all kinds? Ever feel the tug or nibble of a fish at the end of a line? Well he bit.

"So, what happened to him, some sort of *Touched By An Angel* thing?" he asked, referring to a primetime television show that depicts angels interacting with humans in dramatic fashion.

"Bigger," I said.

About 10 seconds of time went by, but it seemed like at least 30 as I awkwardly sipped my Coke... "Well, if you don't mind me asking, can you tell me the story?" he pressed.

Inside, I thought, "okay, tuck your toes in, because here I come!"

And so, I yelled the testimony of my father, Lloyd Barker, who had moved to our little town of 100 Mile House, B.C. in 1969-70 from the streets of Vancouver to sober up after some 30 years of alcoholism. He was skid row material, a derelict, drinking anything and everything. Vanilla extract was not below his dignity he used to say. Sobering up didn't work. He became our town drunk—you know, the guy you see stumbling in a ditch late at night, or sitting on a curb during the day, dirty, gaunt and unshaven... that was my dad. I was about 10 or 11 at the time. He spent most of his time in the very bar that we were now sitting in, slept in a cabin up the highway a few kilometers.

One night he stumbled into the back of a local church, a church not known for having anything out of the ordinary ever happen, until that particular weekend that is. There was a traveling evangelist in town, and he was holding some meetings at this little church.

My dad, drunk as a… (Do skunks really get drunk?) town drunk can be, found his way into a back pew and fell asleep during the sermon. He got up and left about three-quarters of the way through the service, and drove his old car to a cabin where his friends were partying.

The story goes that the evangelist asked some of the church elders who that man was. They told him, "Oh that's Lloyd Barker," and basically indicated he was a lost cause. "That man needs to be set free!" the evangelist exclaimed to them, and asked them to find him and bring him in for prayer. It was early the following morning that they drove their van into the driveway where my father was staying. They didn't know that during the previous night, he had tried to commit suicide but the Lord had mercifully prevented it. He had parked his Chevy by the side of the highway, lifted the hood and stood in front of the car. He was simply waiting for a semi-truck to come by and he would push himself out into the path of it. He said he had totally given up on life, had failed his wife and five kids, had failed his God (given his life to Christ at age 11), failed everything—the devil was out to destroy this man and was nearly successful. Despite this highway being the main corridor between Vancouver and the north, which has about 10 eighteen-wheelers a minute passing through, not a single truck came by for over 20 minutes that night. Dad said he felt like even more of a failure because he couldn't even succeed at taking his own life. He was completely in despair. Later, he would say that God held up the traffic that night, just for him.

He recalled the men driving up to the cabin. "They looked like giants," he said. And they told him, "You're coming with us, Lloyd."

He didn't argue but was helped into the van. He said he was so weak, not having eaten for days. Back at the church, they took my dad into a small room where this evangelist simply asked him one question... "Who are you?"

"I'm Satan," dad said in a voice that wasn't his own. It was deep and guttural and took the deacons by surprise.

"Well, whoever you are," the evangelist commanded, "you come out of him right now in the name of Jesus!' And, to the amazement of the wide-eyed deacons watching this drama unfold, Dad shrieked and convulsed, his wine-stained shirt literally ripping in shreds off his back, top to bottom, as he was set free by the resurrection power of Jesus Christ, the risen, strong and Almighty Son of God!
Dad was literally set free! He never, ever touched a drink again, nor even craved one for the rest of his earthly life, almost 20 years of freedom. (Later he

was also healed of angina, where he needed a triple bypass one day, and the next day, he didn't.)

Needless to say, he was a guy who loved to tell his story as he was forgiven much so he loved much. His favorite song was the old hymn *He Touched Me*. So, like I said, there I was, in the bar, telling the story now to David as I told it above, and David's eyes were becoming quite large.

Dad's story naturally leads into my own testimony of drug and alcohol abuse, and how God rescued me out of that, put my life back on solid ground, and… "Oh," I said, "I forgot to tell you what I do now. I'm the pastor at Cariboo Christian Life Fellowship (CCLF) here in town." Well, he gathered up his chin from the floor and looked at me for a bit. He then asked the obvious question that others had been asking all night. "So, what are you doing here?"

"Well, I believe God speaks today, though people don't always hear Him. Sometimes He speaks to me through dreams." I then told him my dream about the Lord searching for people in bars and parties. "That is why I am here. God is searching for you." Believe it or not, he said, "I think He is." He then told me how he was raised as an agnostic-near-atheist but the last few months he has been thinking more about God. How cool was that!

In fact, he had prayed to God for the first time on his trip from Toronto to 100 Mile House in order to get through a snowstorm, and God had answered that prayer. He then had met a waitress in town who gave him a Bible, which he had begun to read. He had some questions about some of the things he was reading.

I don't know about you, but sometimes I listen to people and carry on another conversation in my head at the same time (horizontally and vertically). This time I was listening to him ask me questions and at the same time, marveling at how the Lord had set this up. I was praising the Lord for the perfect timing in all of this and how He led me here, this particular night, at this particular bar, to this particular table, to speak to this particular young man. WOW!

I answered his questions. He drove me home. I asked if I could pray with him, and he said he would like that, and so our relationship began.

The next week I was prayer-walking again and asking the Lord about being led by His Spirit, and for some examples of when I have done that. The Lord said to me clearly, "remember the dream and the bar." (Even as I write this I marvel at His great grace in my life.)

"Oh yes, I can't forget David," I was thinking. "That was pretty cool, Father." My thoughts then went to David and I wondered if he might be interested in coming to a Christian men's conference with my son, Dustin, and I. Dustin was

near his age, and it would seem more appropriate...
I was thinking about this, then arguing with myself
(ever do that?) that David was a journalist and
would probably be very busy on the weekend... and
what's more he is sort of an atheist, he said, and...
and... I was going over excuses in my head when
suddenly I realized I had just walked past the man
outside a local store!

"Hey Rick!"

"David!" I said.

"Hey I was just thinking about you," he said.

Inside I was marveling again at the Lord's
incredible timing.

"Really? I was just thinking about you!"

"Oh?" he says. What about?" That was his
investigative journalist training coming out, no
doubt.

So, I just bluntly asked him, "Well... I was
wondering if ... you might want to come to a
Christian men's conference...with Dustin and I...?"

"Sure," he said.

"Sorry?"

He confirmed to me that yes, he was sure he would like to go and he has the time off to do it. Incredible.

It was at that men's conference that a speaker, a former NHL hockey player, gave his testimony of how he came to know Jesus, and the invitation to accept Christ as Savior and Lord. I watched in some measure of shock as David mouthed the prayer in the stands and looked very sincere doing it. I kept thinking that was all too easy; it all fell together, and there was no strain whatsoever!

I asked him several times that weekend, "So are you really in, or…?" He assured me that he was definitely in, and in fact, not two weeks later, he himself cast some demons out of a man! Oh, he was in, baby! He was as in as in could be! He was so studious in the Bible that it amazed me. He lapped up the scripture, testified all the time to everyone he could, and lived out his new-found faith with sincerity, never wanting to turn to the left or to the right. Oh – and that waitress that gave him the Bible – they ended up marrying and serving the Lord in another community some three hours away. That was a great story as it unfolded, though the story is not over. David and his wife went through some hard times later in their marriage and ended up separating. Just goes to show that one always needs to abide in the Savior and the truth of His word – abide, dwell, live, reside (not just Sunday morning) or you might become vulnerable to the enemy's tactics.

But as far as the harvesting went, the truth is, it was easy. It was all the Lord (which is why I know the story is not over because the Lord is faithful to complete that which He started in someone's life). The Lord was the One searching. He was the One leading. He knew David before I did. He led that night to the bar where David was; He led me to that particular table, to that particular young man that He had already been working on. David had already been on a journey, was already asking the questions; the Holy Spirit had already been drawing him, and I simply stepped into the Lord's timing and picked a very ripe apple off the tree. It really was amazing.

I think we can learn some things from this. The harvest is indeed ripe. Jesus also said, "My Father is always at work," and we can join Him in that work. He speaks today; we need to listen.

He said His sheep know His voice. We need to pray and to listen. We need to act; we need to dare to take risks, getting out of our comfort zone, off the sidelines and into the game. Whether it is sowing seed, watering, cultivating or reaping, we can have joy doing it as we participate in the Father's rescue missions, the greatest rescue mission of all time – to seek and to save that which was lost. Let's look for those divine interruptions in our day and always be alert for our opportunity to make the most of every opportunity! This is not something that only pastors can do or the paid professionals. This is for all who name Jesus as Lord. He invites us to participate with Him in the greatest rescue mission ever launched.

And I guess that begs the question: how do I know this is really God speaking to me?

Going deeper...

1) Good question, how do we know when it is God speaking?
2) What are some of the ways we can confirm it is God speaking to us and not just the pizza from the night before?
3) Why is it important to have the Bible as the final means of authority for the decisions we make each day?
4) What does it mean to 'join Jesus' in the work He is doing?
5) How do we recognize that work and how do we join in?
6) Jesus said the harvest is ripe. Pray for laborers. When we pray for laborers, do you think Jesus is hoping we might also be the answer to our own prayers?

Chapter 3
A Funny Thing Happened to Me on the Way to a Coffee...

"My sheep know my voice." ~ Jesus, John 10:16

Who would have thought that God cared about my little Ford Tempo?

But you know what? God does care about the things you care about. I cared about my car, even if it was a clunker.

I was in youth ministry back then and was in the city of Kamloops at a youth convention. I was parked at a local fast food joint, started with an M and ended in 2,500 calories. I was waiting for my teens to get their food and come out.

I was happy. I had everything I needed, namely my burger, my fries and my shake.

Then out of the blue comes the thought: "I should park over there," looking at an empty parking stall across the lot. Then that old argument began. "Why would I want to park over there? Why can't I just stay here; there's no reason to go moving the car now. The teens won't be able to find me... I think that's just stupid..."

That's when I saw it.

I glanced up in my rearview mirror and noticed a truck backing out of a stall behind me. I realized the driver did not see my car; he was going to back right into me! I must do something! Must do something now! I put my burger on the dash, spilled my milkshake in the process and "meeped" my little horn. Too late.

FHUMP! The sound of scraping metal sent a shiver up my spine and moved me forward in my seat. I steadied my milkshake but cringed at the hit as the driver turned around in disbelief; his bumper drove right into my trunk, denting it up and leaving a nice permanent reminder of the scriptures that say, "he who has an ear, let him hear."

Sigh. After the dust had settled, I remembered my little argument I had had inside my head, inside my mind, will and emotions (soul) about moving my car.

Now wait just a minute! Was that God Who suggested I move my Tempo? Did He care about my little clunker of a car? Could it be? Could God be speaking to me about things like that?

The obvious answer to that question is: You bet!

I am reminded of the scripture I quoted earlier from the Book of Job, "God does speak, now one way, now another, though men may not perceive it." The trick is in the perceiving it. He who has an ear, let him hear. Does that mean that even those who have ears, may *not* hear? Yup.

Right after that car incident, I decided to try to pay attention to the Lord interrupting my thoughts and speaking to me daily. I mean I really wanted to hear Him. I really wanted to learn to listen, without going off the deep end, or becoming parked in section whacko, Flakesville, Psychoworld or the land of make believe.

Two days later, I was back in my hometown, had dropped off my son, Dustin and my daughter, Denai, at school, and was going to the corner store to pick up a coffee before heading to the office.

I noticed a little old lady out near her car at the gas pumps. I didn't take too much notice but the thought struck me to ask her if she needed any help because she looked a little perplexed. But did I? No. Because I thought that would be a bit rude and presumptuous of me (arguing again) and besides why would she be out there at the gas pump if she didn't know what to do? So, I decided to mind my own business, went in, got my coffee, came out and found she was still there standing and staring at the pumps.

Now I couldn't resist. Why should I mind my own business when I should be about my Father's business?

"Do you need help?" I yelled across the parking lot as I opened my car door.

She nodded yes, and so I put my coffee on the roof of my car and went over.

You know what she said? Of course, you don't. I'll tell you.

"My husband just died," she said. "He never taught me how to use one of these things." She started to cry and I realized that again, wow, this is a Kingdom moment and I had almost missed it.

So, I taught her how to use the self-serve pump, told her I was a pastor and asked if I could pray. It was a great time of ministry – which would not have happened, had I listened to the "spirit-of-stupid" argument that was going on inside my head. You must step out, and you have to take risks. Faith is spelled RISK. You must dare. Why not? What's the worst thing that could happen? That what I always ask now, and usually my answer is, "well, they could kill me, but then, hey! I will be in heaven, so it's all good!"

Later that same week at that same corner store, I went in to get my coffee before going to the office. The thought came in to my head, "I should pick up a Tribune this morning."

Now you must understand that I almost *never* read the Tribune; it is not our local paper; it is from another small community and for the most part, I could care less about what the Tribune should offer. When I was a journalist, it was our rival paper, so I had a bit of a bias about the whole thing. But on that day, I get this thought about picking it up. I looked at it, the front-page headline said nothing that interested me.

I looked at it.

I even touched it. Then the clerk said, "Will that be all?"

"Yes," I said, and walked out with just my coffee in hand.

I arrived at the office as usual and just as I was coming in, the phone was ringing. I picked it up with a hearty "G'd morning, CCLF, Pastor Rick here..." There was an older lady on the other end who was crying because she was (I learned in a few moments) grieving the loss of her grandchild.

Do you know what she asked me? DO YOU KNOW WHAT SHE ASKED ME?!

"Have you seen the paper this morning?"

I cringed inside as I asked her, "which paper?" And yup, you know it, it was the Tribune. You see, on the cover of the Tribune, bottom half of the broadsheet paper tucked under, was a picture of her grand-daughter who had just recently died.

Now, had I picked up the Trib, and read that story first, I would not have had to put this loving grandma through the story all over again.

I could have said, "Yes, yes I know all about it," and simply just ministered to her need. But no, that time, I didn't listen to the still, small voice; instead I listened to my loud, overbearing argument that is anchored in fleshly pride – me, me, me. I repented before the Lord for this one and for all the other times when I failed to listen.

You might think that this was a small, trivial thing. But not to that wee grandmother – and not to the Lord! He cares about what people care about deep inside. He longs to have compassion on people, delighting over them with singing, wanting to quiet them with His love (Zephaniah 3:17).

Oh no, it may be a small thing in our eyes but God sees with a different perspective. And so I note the stakes are high in obedience. Give me another opportunity Lord, just to hear Your voice, and obey.

And He has given me more opportunities, some I have failed at, and some I have obeyed in. The times of obedience have always resulted in blessing, even if it wasn't obvious that another person was ministered to. I was blessed in my obedience, for sometimes I know He asks us to do things simply to see if we obey. It is part of our growing up into maturity in the Lord.

Like the time I was in Vancouver and I had been to a friend's church. The pastor had preached about always being ready, in season and out, to tell your story. At the end of the service, he brought us into a place of quiet, and he said, "Let God bring to your mind a name of someone. Perhaps you are to tell this person your story."

The name "David" literally popped to my mind. Now at that time, all the Davids I knew were Christians, so I sort of shrugged my shoulders and dismissed the thought, although it did cross my mind that maybe I would meet a David. So, I prayed. "Lord if you want me to speak to a David, send me a David."

That was rather a bold prayer now that I think of it.

Well, a lot of funny things happen to me on the way to a coffee. Just sayin'…

I pulled into a corner store, same chain as in my hometown, to grab a coffee (okay okay I know that it's getting obvious) and I was in line at the counter when my heart began to pound! It wasn't the caffeine or lack of it. The clerk had a nametag on, and yes, printed on the nametag in letters that appeared to be three-dimensional as they leapt out and enlarged before my eyes was: *David.*

My first instinct was to set the coffee down and just get out of there. But c'mon! I had just prayed that prayer!

He was a dark young man, probably of African descent and looked to be around 18 years old. I thought, "Gee, I wonder if he knows Swahili…"

Wha?! Why would I think that?
I mean that is a silly thing to wonder, because I don't wonder that every time I run into an African American. This time though, the thought struck me hard. And I couldn't shake it.

You see, I know a little Swahili because a wonderful brother in the Lord, who was from Ethiopia, taught me some common words and phrases, telling me that, "one day you will need it."

As I moved closer to it being my turn at the counter, the inner argument amped up. "Don't be stupid. Why do you think he'd know Swahili? He's a teenager; he's not interested in what you have to say. He just wants to take your money and get on with his day…" and so on.

It was almost my turn. I noticed on David's left wrist was a bracelet and on the bracelet, were some strange words.
"Hi," he said. "Will that be all?"
"Yup, hey, what does your bracelet mean?"
"Oh," he said. "That is my name." And then he added it: "in Swahili."

Inside my heart is going BA-BAM! I again marvel at how the Lord does this, if we simply let Him!

"Jumbo Endugo (phonetically) Habadi Yacko?"
meaning "Hi Brother, how are you?"

Well, this dude's eyeballs almost popped out of his
head as he looked at this white boy who was now
speaking his native language! Unbelievable! You
know the Lord struck up a conversation there that
was awesome. I had told him that I didn't think our
meeting was an accident but that God brought us
together for some reason. In a matter of minutes, he
literally unloaded to me all about his life, his
struggles, and about his mother who was very ill,
and in need of physical healing. I couldn't believe
how open he was to receive ministry in the name of
the Lord Jesus Christ. And all I came in there for
was a coffee. At least that is what I thought.

Now I would love to say, "and then David knelt
down right there in the middle of the store and gave
his life to Jesus," but that didn't happen. In fact, I
never saw him again after that, but you know what,
the story's not over. This David is just like that
other David, whom I met in the bar, on a separate
journey, to the Father of Lights. An old saying goes,
"The Providence of God will always lead you to the
God of Providence." So, I believe one day, I will
see David again, and he will know the Lord, and
may even testify about how one day as an 18-year-
old clerk, there was this guy who came in and told
him about Jesus.
So, back to that question, "Well, how do you know?
How do you know whether it's God or just you?"

Great question. I guess in reality, you don't know right off. The more you step out though, the more you begin to recognize the voice of the Holy Spirit. Jesus said the Holy Spirit would lead you, would speak to you, and would even show you of things to come. He is your personal Tutor and He will never, ever tell you to do something that goes against the written revelation of God's Holy Word, the Bible. In addition, He will always magnify the Son of God, Jesus Christ. That's His mandate. That's His job, And He does it very well.

People ask, "But does He speak in the first person or second person?"

Hey, He's God. He can do what He likes. He can do both. For me, He often speaks in the first person, meaning I will get a thought that is like, *"I should do this, or I should do that; I should pick up that hitchhiker; I should talk to that lady, I should buy a Tribune; I should clean the sink, do the dishes..."* Now I can hear some of you guys out there going, "wait a minute, don't get carried away!"

But I say, "oh yes, DO get carried away! But always use the Bible as your Plumb-line of accuracy. Listen to the Lord help you become a better husband, a kinder, gentler person, a godly man, a man of integrity. If God is whispering in your ear to clean the sink after you shave, clean the sink! And thank God that He is teaching to be a better husband. Oh, and don't blow it by saying, "hey honey, look I cleaned the sink!" It really is that simple.

As I said earlier, I have had many opportunities where I have missed the boat, and missed the opportunity to step out of the boat. I see it in hindsight and realize, "oops that was God." But the more we experience Him, the more we love Him, and the more we love Him, the more we will want to obey Him, and the more we obey Him, the more we will experience Him, and the more we experience Him, the more we love Him, and the... you get the picture.

Going deeper...

1) Have you ever experienced God nudging you or speaking to you outside of church?

2) What was that like? Was it in the first-person voice of "I should do this or that..." or was it more like "YOU, GO HERE..."

3) Why would we say, 'faith is spelled R.I.S.K'?

4) When was the last time you stepped out in risk and said something to a stranger?

5) When was the last time you said to someone, 'can I pray for you... right now?" And then did it.

6) Can you think of a New Testament story when someone was obedient to the nudges of God, not knowing what the whole picture was, but just taking the next step?

7) What are three ways to test whether it is God speaking to you or not?

Chapter 4
Kiss the Bear

Consider it pure joy my brethren when you fall into various trials, knowing that the testing of your faith produces patience. – James 1:2-3

Ever been chased by an overbearing, growling old grizzly bear? I have.

Pastoral ministry, as you know, has its ups and downs. Statistics show outrageous amounts of pastors leave the ministry each month, most suffer burnout; many feel they can't cut it, and that being a pastor adversely affects their family. Sigh.

Sometimes a pastor is so totally amazed at the graciousness of the people he is called to serve, and at other times... well, other times remind me of a 93-year-old pastor who stood up at a pastor's conference and said in a cranky old voice, "after 50 years of ministry, I have learned one thing – sheep bite!"

That's a BLT of ministry. A leader buddy of mine named Pat Melanson, a good friend who has walked with me through tremendous waters under many bridges, coined that term and we laugh out loud when we talk about our BLTs (bottom line theology).

"Life sucks, but God is good," he'd say. That's a BLT. We have many more. One time he added on to the "sheep bite" statement. He said, "yup and sometimes *sheepbite* can be fatal, which is why the Lord gives shepherds those staffs – not to scare wolves away, but to bat the sheep!"

Perhaps you need to be a pastor to laugh at that but I think you understand.

Just before a period of time in my life that seemed to be full of sheep bites, goat butts and donkey kicks, not to mention a few of those wolves lurking around, I had a series of three dreams involving the exact same characters, in particular, two massive grizzly bears.

The first dream I thought was just an interesting dream about two bears, one that was off doing its own thing, feeding on some bugs under a stump, and then there's this other bear, which I knew was a big ol' male that swung its head toward me and starts running right at me!

When it started running, I started running! I ran to my car, which of course like in any good dream, was locked. You can picture the scene, fumbling with my car keys, bear getting closer, me looking over my shoulder, bear getting closer, fumbling, closer. I finally get the door open, jump into the seat and slam the door shut just as the great beast KABASHES my car by slamming into the side of it. I lay a strip of rubber as I peel away in my car, noticing in my rearview mirror that out of my trunk, a duffel bag flew open and a bunch of baggage was strewn all over the road. The last thing I recall of that dream was the bear pawing at my baggage.

I awoke from that, noting it, jotting it down in my journal but not really paying too much attention to it.

Until two nights later, when I had another dream. Same sort of scene unfolded – two bears, one eating away minding its own business, the other picking up my scent, swinging its big head about, then coming after me from across a field.

That's when I began to pay attention. I felt that these dreams may be from the Lord, that He was inviting me into a time of seeking Him for the answers to the riddle of the dreams. What did these two bears represent? Why was one chasing me and the other not? What was going on?

Then I had the third dream.

I remember it so vividly because it felt very real. I was out in the woods in a weathered ramshackle little cabin, looking out what was once a framed window but now was just a bit of a hole in the wall. And there they were.

Two bears, same grizzlies, one eating away like nothing was the matter, and the other suspiciously sniffing the air. It was as if it knew the exact moment that I had noticed it. It lifted its massive head, swung it madly in my direction and started coming, lofting its way toward me!

I pulled away from the window and looked around the cabin. There was nothing to use as a weapon! It wasn't long before I could hear the bear right outside the door, snorting and sniffing and whoofing about. I moved toward the window hole as the bear smashed its way through the door and came barreling into the one-room cabin! I jumped out the window and scrambled. I mean I scrambled! Looking behind me as I tried to get away and get up from the ground as quickly as possible, I noticed the bear was coming out the window, pearly white teeth snapping, fiercely growling away. It was like the window had expanded to allow the bear through! So, I timed my escape and as soon as it came halfway out the window, I went around and back in through the broken down door! We did this a few times like in a cartoon, out the window, in the door, out the window, in the door, me first, bear behind (no pun intended).

Then I just took off running through the woods but that obsessive bear kept charging. It was serious!

I was panicking at this point because all around me were those wispy little aspen trees, nothing to climb at all. Have you ever tried running in your dreams only to find you're just going in really slow motion or you just can't… seem… to… move? It was like that.

I stopped and turned around to face the bear. I stood behind a stupid little aspen tree about three inches in diameter as if this would offer some protection. The bear kept coming, head moving up and down with each stride, saliva spraying from its mouth, its jowls going in and out like in slow motion. I could even smell its breath as it got closer. Rancid.

In desperation and fear I yelled out to heaven, "GOD, WHAT DO I DO?!!"

Believe it or not a voice came from heaven, very clearly and I knew it to be God. It was a solid, deep, very calm voice that could only be God.

"KISS THE BEAR."
"WHAT?!"
Again, it came. *"Kiss the bear."*
So, that's what I did.
Yeah, I kissed the bear. I grabbed that bear's face by its jowls and plunked a big ol' smack right on its snout.

The big bruin reared back with a stunned look on its face, and gave out a surprised, woofy, deep kind-of-grunt that only a grizzly bear could give. It sort of sounded like *Scooby Doo* going "huhhhhh?"

And then it dropped to the ground in utter defeat, and literally disintegrated! That's when I awoke

Actually, I woke up with laughter. I was laughing and asking God what in the world does all this mean?

Over the next week, I asked a lot of people their thoughts about the dream and about the characteristics and habits of grizzly bears. I got books about grizzlies and what they are like; I scanned our dream interpretation books that suggested bears represent the enemy, bad things, etc., etc. but I did not feel that it was clear what God was trying to say. Kiss the enemy? I don't think so.

About two weeks went by and I was sitting in my office asking the Lord, "Okay, what are You trying to say to me?"

And then it came. I began to write down my thoughts and it made perfect sense.

"The two bears represent two *places* in your life, one of contentment (the bear that was eating) and feeding upon the nutrients provided for you (in the Word particularly) and the other place is a *place* of unpredictability and fear. Embrace that place; kiss the bear. Welcome it for it is a place of faith, and a place of learning. Be like King David who learned how to behave in the cave, who learned how to survive in the desert, to find water, to find food and sustenance, and how to fight. Kiss the bear."

What a wonderful God to communicate to me that I was about to enter into a time of unpredictability and fear! And that is exactly what happened. I went through a period of testing and trying at the hands of Christian people (sheepbite) but through it all, I realized that I was to welcome this time because the Lord was kind enough to be teaching me; the Lord was testing me, and the Lord would sustain me.

I had a fourth dream about a grizzly some months later. It was a hand-to-paw combat dream, a fight with the creature that was twice my size, and twice as loud and nasty… but I won. No weapons but my bare hands and I killed the bear.

So, there was a time to kiss the bear and a time to kill the bear.

When it was done, I looked down in my dream and noticed that my legs were all scarred up. I was not in pain and there was no blood to speak of. I was just scarred for life.

In processing this fourth dream, I realized that I had been wounded in the strength of my legs, the strongest portion of my physical body. I think the Lord was saying I will have wounds and scars and will "bear the marks" (pun intended) of the battle in the strongest part of my ministry at that time. And, that is indeed what took place. Hard as it was, the fact would remain that I won the fight in the strength of the Lord; the bear was defeated and I was to move on.

So, whatever you might be going through or facing may seem overwhelming and fearful, but I invite you to *kiss the bear*, to welcome a time like this, because it is in the desert times that God speaks so tenderly to us (Hosea 2:14). And those desert times are character shapers, showing us what we would not know otherwise.

By the way, to cap off this story, God in His great humor, planned something just for me to enjoy.

Marci and I were in Scotland on a ministry trip some time later when I came across one of those tourist sites that sell various kinds of kilts, tartans and swords, plaster your name on key chains and plaques, showing what the name means and so on. I found the name "Barker" which surprised me somewhat.

It was the only one in the entire store, and the only one I'd ever seen before or since – a little cardboard wall hanging that explained the history of the Barker name. I think I actually heard God chuckle when I read that the armorial bearings of the name "Barker" was in fact the head of a bear, well, three of them to be exact, and that reminded me of the three dreams God gave me to warn me of a time to come. I also noted that the head of the bear was no longer on its body -- decapitated.

I could just imagine God leaning over to Peter and saying, "watch this Peter; this will be good."

What a setup; just one plaque with Barker on it, in just one store in the middle of the Scottish countryside that I just happen to stop in at for a bathroom break and to look at some souvenirs.

Nice touch, Lord. Nice touch.

You're the best!

Going deeper...

1) Do you have one or two lifetime BLT's that you can share?
2) Do you keep a journal?
3) Do you recall your dreams when you wake up?
4) Do you take your dreams seriously? Having a paper and pen beside your bed to jot notes from a dream can be of good assistance.
5) Paying attention to your dreams, writing them down, seeking God for interpretations could be a gateway to some new adventures in God. Are you willing to listen?
6) What are some Biblical stories that include God using dreams to speak to His people?
7) Look at Job 33:14 – do you think God still speaks in dreams today? Why or why not?

Chapter 5
Duh! The Sound of Revelation

"...this was not revealed to you by man, but by my Father in heaven." – Matthew 16:17

I'm about to tell you one of the most profound things I have ever heard, or said, and when you hear it, you'll go, "Well duh!"

Are you ready?

You might want to sit down, grab a coffee, breathe a deep breath and really wrap your mind around this. I mean when you hear it and let it sink into your system, you might really launch something new. Your life may never be the same again. This could change the way you do your job, even how you look at life in general. It might even change the way you live, period. Are you ready for it? Are you, huh, are you?

I mean if you really get a hold of this, you'll probably never be the same. It's one of those phrases that just sticks to you like peanut butter on bread. I mean… okay, okay, here it is: I mean this was such a revelation to me that I slapped my forehead and said, "Well duh!" – okay, okay, here it is.

If you always do what you've always done, you'll always get what you've always had."

C'mon, read it again, slowly. Think about it now. Some people go through life and never think to change. One of the definitions of insanity is to continually do the same thing over and over again, while expecting a different result. But really, if you always do what you've always done, you'll always get what you've always had.

You might say, "Well duh," and that really is the sound of revelation when it hits your spirit, but if it is so simple, why is it that so many Christians never get out of the flippin' rut they've been in for 25 years? They know the truth, yet they still do the same things over and over and over again. Apparently, a road sign on the Alaskan Highway used to say, "be careful how you choose your rut; you'll be in it for the next 200 miles," and a rut in a Christian life is really a grave with the ends knocked out.

So, consider your life. If you don't like what you're getting, it is time to try something different. If you don't like your prayer life, try something different, getting up earlier, staying up later, prayer walking, or prayer-journaling, whatever, just do something about it.

If you aren't sensing the Lord's tangible presence in your day to day, get-up-and-go-to-work day, then try something different! If you're a preacher and the well is dry, try something different. It takes risk; it takes faith. We must adjust because if we always do what we've always done, we'll always get what we've always had.

If Abraham didn't risk leaving everything he had ever known to follow after a God he'd just met, history would have been very, very different. But instead, against all odds, hope against hope, the Bible says, he believed God and it was credited to him as righteousness.

What if Zacchaeus had done what he always had instead of climbing up that sycamore tree? What if blind Bartimaeus hadn't risked everything to scream out, "Jesus, Son of David, have mercy on me!"? What if Gideon decided to just stay put and continue grinding wheat in the wine press? What if Jehu decided to ignore Elisha's call, and go on playing cards instead of driving his chariot like a madman and taking out Jezebel? What if Peter hadn't followed the angel of prison? What if the church hadn't prayed? What if? What if? What if?

What if you don't take the opportunity God is giving you to step out in faith, believe Him and do that thing that He has been talking to you about? If you always do what you've always done, you'll always get what you've always had.

Revelation from God is not complicated.

So often when God speaks to me, He tells me simple truths that when I get them, I think, "Well of course… why didn't I see that before?" Then I slap\ my forehead and say "DUH!"

Revelation is in fact the foundation of how Jesus builds His church. Remember the story in the Gospels where Jesus is asking the boys "Guys, who do people say I am?" And, in their brilliance, they responded that some called him a prophet, some Elijah, others Jeremiah. Then he asked them, "Okay, but who do you say I am?"

It was ol' Pete who caught something there, and you can almost see him gasping, pointing at Jesus and saying, "I know, I know! You are the Christ, the Son of the Living God!!"

Jesus smiles and winks, and says, "Aha! Flesh and blood didn't reveal that to you Peter, but my Father in heaven did. Upon this rock, I will build my church and the gates of hell shall not prevail against it!"

Well of course, a lot of people have mistakenly figured that Peter himself is the rock that Christ was talking about there because his name means "rock" but I believe the rock Jesus was referring to was the rock of revelatory information, hidden treasures of understanding given by the Father Himself through the Spirit – particularly that knowledge that Jesus is the Son of the Living God! "Upon this rock, I will build my Church!"

So how does that work? It's simple. Revelation through the Spirit to the spirit. You know that we are triune beings, right? We are created in the image of God, the Triune God Who is Three – Father, Son and Holy Spirit. He designed the Tabernacle for the Israelites to represent that too – outer court, inner court, holy of holies – three in one. We are also made up of three parts – spirit, soul and body. The soul, consisting of our mind, will and emotions, cannot seem to process revelation from the Spirit of God. The soul process information, process logic, processes feelings and choices, but the spirit alone – and only one that is quickened and made alive by belief in Jesus – is what can really handle revelation from God.

Where does God dwell when someone becomes born again? In their spirit. He doesn't dwell in your earlobe or right wrist (body), doesn't dwell in your brain (thoughts) or emotions and personality (soul). The spirit of a man is where God dwells when you invite Him into your life. As a result, our spirit is always in the presence of the Lord and it is our spirit that processes His revelation. That's why you can read a Bible passage that you have read for years and then all of a sudden… BAM! The revelation of it hits your spirit and you never, ever, ever forget it again. That revelation then is worked out through your soul and through your body as you apply it. First there is the revelation and then there's the opportunity to work it out, or put it into practice.

Take Peter for example who in Acts 10 had a revelatory experience and then the opportunity to put into practice that which he understood. He fell into a trance, which by the way, many Christians today would say, "Oh that couldn't be God then," and he sees a vision of heaven opened up and something like a large sheet being let down to earth by its four corners. It contained all kinds of four-footed animals and reptiles as well as birds. Then a voice told him, "Get up Peter, kill and eat."

His initial response was to the effect of, "I don't think so! Are you crazy? These are impure, unclean things and I have never eaten anything impure!"

The voice says – and by the way, the Greek word used for voice here means to 'disclose, to show, to enlighten or to shine' – the voice warns Peter not to call anything impure that God has made clean. This experience happens three times, which makes me relate to Peter in a way, as it often takes at least three times before he gets something… three denials, three reinstatements, three visions. For me it is more like 10 times but we're talking about Peter here.

While Peter is still wondering and pondering about this incredible vision of impure vs. pure, the three men that God had already instructed the Gentile Cornelius through an angelic visitation to send to Peter (I love it how God works on so many different levels) showed up at his door. Yeah, He is always doing more behind the scenes that we can see Him doing right in front of our noses.

Peter invites them in, which was already more than a little bit of a no-no in his very orthodox Jewish culture, and the next day sets out with them to go to Cornelius' house to share with them the gospel. He must have been thinking all along, "This makes no sense whatsoever; I know that I should not be doing this. I cannot figure it out. Why would God call something clean when it has already been ruled unclean? But I know that was God speaking… I must be obedient."

So often, we try to figure everything out *first* before we obey but God usually leads us into the ridiculous, the ludicrous so that we can walk by faith not by sight. We used to sing that old hymn "Trust and Obey" but lately I've been thinking we might want to change it to Obey and Trust. Obey first, trust the Lord and He'll work everything out. I suppose in reality they overlap one another Trust and Obey. Obey and Trust.

So, Peter had an opportunity to put into practice the word that God was speaking to him. He gave him a revelation that was very new and now he had to put it into practice. Paul says in the letter to the Romans that "faith comes by hearing and hearing the Word of God." And now after Peter heard the word of God, he needed to walk by faith in it.

Think about Gideon again, David, story after story where people were told to do something and then they had to act upon it. The scripture says faith comes by hearing, not "having heard" that means it is current; it is now; it is actively hearing and heeding the voice of the Lord. Peter told the gathering at the house that they all knew the rules about a Jew associating with a Gentile but then he declares his revelation.

"But God has shown me that I should not call anyone unclean or impure." If Peter went on what he had known from his childhood rather than the current settings on his hard drive, revival never would have happened for the Gentiles.

It wasn't until after Cornelius explained what happened to him, and how God visited him with an angel that Peter basically explained "NOW I GET IT!"

He says, "I now realize how true it is that God does not show favoritism but does what is right."

The rest is remarkable history how the Holy Spirit decides to drop in for a visit there and wreak heavenly havoc among the believers. He shows up big time and has the Gentiles speaking in tongues, and prophesying to the place where it is no point denying what God is doing.

But it was the revelatory work of the Holy Spirit that softened Peter's heart, allowing himself to even walk with a Gentile, and then later to sleep in the home of a Gentile and then later to step foot into one's home and share the one and only enduring, glorious good news of the Lord Jesus Christ. Peter put feet to his faith.

God is very, very sneaky. I respectfully call Him Jehovah Sneaky these days. Perhaps there is a clue that God had something up His sleeve when you consider that Peter was staying at a tanner's house. Hmmmm, that was another cultural no-no! Seems God was already softening up his heart for a lesson.

And you know what, God really does like to speak with us and teach us how to pray in faith. He has given us the Holy Spirit to guide and lead us. He is good to us! He will take us into tough situations so that we can adjust in in faith. He so likes it when we act in faith. I heard someone say recently that **God allows things to happen TO us so that things can happen IN us so that things can happen THROUGH us!**
But while He has been sneaky with me, more often He has just had to talk straight to me and that is like being hit in the side of the head with my own thick, leather-bound Bible. Once I was going through a season of yuck, which I think is a Greek word meaning crap, and I wasn't seeing clearly either. I was frustrated; I know I was angry and tired; I was distracted and drained.
Then God in His graciousness spoke a revelatory word directly to my spirit. I actually knew the

information before in my soul but it wasn't going deep into my core, my spirit.

He said, *"Rick, satan hates you. He hates you and he hates everything you're doing in the kingdom. He hates you with a deep hatred and he wants to take you out."*

Wow! Simple enough alright, but this came at a time when I was wondering why I was going through what I was going through. I had forgotten that I am in a war. I was focused on the wrong things, at the wrong times and when the realization came that this is in fact is a war, I took the revelation and did something about it. I rallied the troops, called for prayer and then great breakthrough came.

Again, it was the revelatory word of God spoken, and then an opportunity to put feet to it, to do something about, to obey.

So, if you always do what you've always done, you'll always get what you've always had. If Peter had dismissed the revelation and had always done what he always had, breakthrough would not have come to the Gentile church. In fact, most of us would not be in the kingdom today.
If you're tired of what you're getting now, get something new by trying something different. Step out. Step out in faith. God likes that and He will meet you in that very moment.

Going deeper…

1) Why is 'revelation' the key to Christ building His Church?

2) What is the difference between our spirit, soul and body?

3) How is a revelatory word spoken in your spirit worked out through your soul (mind, will and emotions) and your body?

4) We know God is omnipresent (everywhere) But where does God the Father dwell according to the Bible? Where does God the Son dwell? Where does God the Spirit dwell?

5) What steps can you take today to enhance your communion with the Holy Spirit inside you?

6) Look at John 14 through 16 taking note of all the aspects of the Holy Spirit's 'job description' that Jesus talks about.

Chapter 6
Ready or Not Here I come...

All the ways of the Lord are loving and faithful for those who keep the demands of His covenant. –
Psalm 25:10

I had my sermon all prepared.

I mean I hadn't preached in about four weeks and had been really working on this one. It was called "Ready or Not, Here I come." Brilliant I thought!

I even had notes printed in the bulletin. I'm not usually a three-point sermonator but it even had three points to ponder about how God surprises us sometimes.

First point was about the return of Christ. When is He coming back? Your proper response would be "soon!" Right. So, I was going to talk about the return of Christ in the first point, using Matthew 24 and 25 about the way the world is shaping up – yet we're not to be frightened. There is a date set; there will be a marriage supper of the Lamb; there will be a wedding. It will happen. God will do as his Word declares. God has it all under control. So, ready or not, here I come – that was point numero uno.

Point number two was how He is about to come to the corporate church, based on the letters to the seven churches in Revelation, and how in almost all of them He says, "I will come to you." But he is talking about a coming that is one of judgement and it's a bit scary because He says He will come and remove our lamp-stand unless we start dealing with some things in our lives, such as the idolatry which He referred to when He spoke about the Nicolaitans. I was going to get my wife, Marci, to share about some thoughts she had on crafted images that people struggle with in their lives and that are ungodly, and how God was saying, "Ready or Not, Here I Come in regards to idolatry. She has amazing revelation from the Lord on some of these things and I love to hear her speak.

Point three was going to be about our personal lives, and how God does a sneak attack and comes to us and surprises us when we least expect Him. Even in the return of the Lord, He says it will be at a time when you don't expect Him. He'll come then. I considered the guys on the road to Emmaus and how Jesus walked with them when they weren't expecting Him to, and how they didn't even recognize Him until He disappeared. Suuuurprise!

So, I had all this prepared, and then… He surprised me. He did the very thing I was going to talk about! He surprised me with His presence on the Friday before the sermon, and I began to get this phrase pounding in my spirit over and over again – and the more I thought it, the more revelatory it became to me, building my faith. It's about God *not* being taken by surprise at all by anything or anyone but that indeed He has the whole world in His hands. So, I chucked out the three-point sermon and delivered this word: "The story's not over until God says it's over and God will have the last laugh."

I just think of the dozens of stories in scripture where God seems to enjoy having the last laugh on His enemies. From the first pages of Genesis right through to Maps… in nearly every chapter, the truth of the statement, "It's not over till God says it's over" comes barreling through. No matter what you go through, no matter what can be thrown at you, the story is not over till it's over, until God says it's over and you know what, God will have the last laugh.

He is so confident in His ability. Our circumstances seem so big, so impossible but they are trivial to the Lord. That's why He can prepare a meal before us in the presence of our enemies. Confidence.

When they were teenagers, I took my kids, Dustin and Denai to a small community outside of Calgary, Alberta on a short ministry trip. We were joining a small team doing some practical things like digging an irrigation ditch, some ministry stuff on the streets and we helped with a church plant outreach effort.

During one of the days, my 14-year-old daughter noticed in a shop window a pair of running shoes that were so "in" that she just had to have them. She begged me with puppy dog eyes and that little pout face, saying "Puhllleeeeeeaassse, Dad?!"

Well, being the good dad that I want to be, I really wanted to get them for her, and being the smart husband I long to be, I immediately phoned home to ask my wife about it. She said, "go for it."

So together, Denai and I went to the store, her almost giddy but of course that would be uncool so she was just really, really, happy. We got there, and to her utter devastation, the shoes were too small, and they were the only pair the store had.
I remember the silence as we walked back to the car. She was so bummed out and had that look on her face that seemed to say, "Nothing *ever* works out for me."

I figured that we'll probably stop at another store somewhere and they'll likely have them, so I smiled and said to Denai, "Hey, the story's not over." We prayed about it and left it at that.

Well we didn't find any in Alberta nor in B.C. where we stopped along the way home and so we came back empty-handed and broken-hearted as far as my daughter was concerned.

Now back at home, the phone rang. It was for Denai. It was one of our youth interns, who called to say that she had some brand new shoes for her to try because they were too small for herself. You guessed it… same exact shoes.

Now as any reasonable father would think, I thought "teachable moment" and I said to my daughter, "don't ever think the story is over until it is over." That was pretty awesome of God to do that for her. Same shoes. Right size. Free.

Think of Jericho, tightly shut up, the citizens of Jericho laughing outrageously at the Israelites from the top of the massive walled city. The soldiers and regular people of Israel quietly marched around the city, looking like complete idiots, until they shouted at the right moment and as a result the walls came crashing down. That's what we call God having the last laugh.

Ask Job. I mean he must have thought it was over when he lost everything that day, and then started breaking out in boils. Was the story over? Nope. The story was not over because God was still on the job (no pun intended) and He turned all the cursing into the abundant blessing and in the end, He gave him double back of all that he had.

Consider ol' Gideon there counting his numbers thinking he might have a chance even though the odds were four to one. Then God tells him to pare down the army until the odds are now 400 to one and not in his favor. Then God gave the instructions to take a pitcher, a torch and a trumpet and wait for the right time to obey the command to break the pitcher, shout a shout out to the Lord and wave the flame. Who had the last laugh? God did it once again as fear struck the enemy's camp and a great victory was won for the Lord.

Think about David facing Goliath, the huge Philistine warrior who laughed his way onto the battlefield when he saw the ruddy little teenager come out to take him on with a sling.

Think of Moses, a stutterer, being told to go and deliver the people of Israel from the mightiest man on the planet… "and oh, Moses, just a minute…here's a stick."

How about Lazarus? Yeah, he was quite dead in the tomb. I mean, it looked pretty over! But the story wasn't over, nope, not until God said it was over and He would indeed have the last laugh.

Just ask Peter. He must have thought the story was over. I mean he denied Christ three times, denied even knowing the man! He cursed. Was the story over? No! Jesus came and reinstated him three times too.

Ask Paul. Look at his spiritual resume. He was stoned, beaten up, in jail, left for dead, shipwrecked. Was the story over during those trials? Nope. Not until God said so.

Ask Jonah in the belly of the whale. Was it over? Then there's the widow's oil that flowed until there was no more emptiness to fill, Samson wiping out more enemies in his death than he did in his life. Though he was blind and a slave, the story wasn't over. Think of the jealous peers of Daniel who snickered when the king had to throw Danny boy into a den of lions, only to end up in there themselves when God saved Daniel from the pride's late-night snack.

Look at David again, anointed King over all Israel. What happened immediately after that? He was living in the caves for many years, some say 13 or more! He must have thought, "well that prophetic word was really off!" He must have thought the story was pretty much over halfway through the fifth year or so. But the story wasn't over because God had a plan and He was working His plan. He laughs at our plans but He is working on His plan.

Go back to the beginning when Adam and Eve fell in the garden and sinned. They must have thought the story was over. But no, God gave them a promise that her seed would crush the enemy serpent's head. So, there was hope. But think of what it must have been like to be escorted out of the Garden.

They had that promise from God and as someone once said, "If you have the promise of God, you have the reality!"

So, here Eve gets pregnant and bears Cain. Woo hoo! At the beginning, they must have believed he was that seed, the promised one of God who would crush the serpent's head. He was just a baby but why wouldn't they think he was the one? Then he got a little older, and they began to wonder. He has some character deficits coming through… a little arrogant, a little rude at times and talk about selfish!

Cain. His name even means "man" and I think he represents the ways of man, trying to work our way into salvation, please God by our own good works. Then Abel comes along. Now hey, Abel was tender in his heart; Abel loved God; maybe he was the promised one! Yes!

And then Cain murders Abel! Think of how Eve must have felt. Downtrodden, in despair, she wondered if the story was over for them. But no, the story wasn't over because God was just getting started and God gave them Seth, their third.

Cain represents man. Abel represents the death of Christ and as I thought about it, I realized that Seth could very well represent the resurrection! New beginnings and a new season came about for Adam and Eve. In fact, when you look at the genealogies, Cain fades out, Abel didn't have a chance to have a genealogy but it is Seth in Luke 2 who is recorded in the history of Jesus – Seth, the son of Adam! He was the one to carry that promise for Eve and for Adam. The story wasn't over after all, not even after there was death, pain and trouble. God brings a Seth into their lives, a new beginning and a new time. He does the same thing in our lives today.

I think of Abraham as good as dead when he was given the promise of Isaac. I mean, he looked at Sarah his wife, thinking, "oy vey, how can this ever happen? We are old and gravity is taking over. Look at us!" Then Sarah gets the idea of giving Hagar, her servant maid, to Abraham (man's ways) but God had a plan and He was working His plan – and then Sarah got pregnant with Isaac and God had the last laugh. Isaac's name means laughter. I used to think it was only because Sarah laughed at the thought of being pregnant, but maybe it was a God laugh at the impossibility of it all. If you read further on in Genesis in chapter 25, after Sarah died, you can marvel with me. We just understood that Abraham was basically dead in his body and could not produce any children but God intervened and Isaac was born. But now after Sarah died a number of years later, we read in Genesis 25 that old Abraham took another wife whose name was Keturah who gave him another child, and then another and then another! Six in all! Yup, six! Hey, the story's not over till it's over and when God wants to have the last laugh, look out! Six more kids. Way to go, God!

He is so faithful! He is so generous. He has us in His hands. Do not worry! Come to Him and allow Him to draw near to you. Let faith rise in you because God is right there in the midst of your storm, in the midst of your trial.

Early in our marriage, I was jobless and a government error (yes, they admitted it) had caused my unemployment insurance cards to be filed out of order, and so the money was not coming in. My son was just a toddler and we needed food and I was angry.

I would walk to the post office, stick the key into our box, turn it with great hope, only to see an empty compartment staring back at me. I would then slam the door shut in frustration because nothing was there. (Slamming a little mail box door by the way, does not satisfy. It's like trying to hang up a cell phone angrily. You can't.) I would have to think of something to say to my poor wife who was at home anticipating some kind of breakthrough good news in our financial situation.

The stress that this whole thing brought was huge. I remember walking through the door and seeing my wife sitting on the floor with our son, looking up at me with hopeful eyes. I shook my head no.

At this point in our life, we were on the edge of serving God. We had made a commitment but we did not get to church often because I had no vehicle. I didn't like hitching rides with others due to pride. I was unemployed. I hated my life.

I grabbed a Bible off the table and these words came out of my mouth: "Do we chuck this thing?"

I actually did; I threw the Bible onto the floor. But even as I tossed it, I realized it was our only hope that somehow, some way God would come through. Right at that moment, Marci and I got down on our knees beside our bed and I remember praying

through tears, "God, this is probably the place you wanted us all along…"
The next day I went to the post office box abounding with great faith and hope. I was so pumped. I knew today was the day of my provision! I turned the key in the box, opened the door and there it was… absolutely nothing!

I almost died right there on the spot. I was immediately angry and confused. I slowly closed the door and walked away toward home. On the way home, simply putting one foot in front of the other, God gave me a revelatory word, actually two words. He usually speaks that way to me, one and two words at a time. I'm thick.

He spoke into my spirit two words: *"Remember Gideon."*

That was all. It came through very strongly in the depths of my spirit though – and remember I wasn't doing all that well in my journey of faith. I was broken. I was angry. I was confused. I was not going to church regularly. I was a mess. And then God spoke.

So, I started to remember Gideon. I recalled the story from my youth, where God pared his army down so that only God could get the glory for a huge victorious battle against a massive army. The odds were greatly stacked against Gideon and yet God came through.

Perhaps God was bringing me to this place where only He would get the glory for providing for me, not the government, not social services, which had already refused me as well due to the fact that I was supposed to be getting my unemployment cheques. I couldn't even rely on my own ability. Only God and God alone. So, I went home again, this time with that word on my lips, and hoped that it would help Marci to have some hope too.

Do you know that in less than two hours that day, I was standing dumbfounded in my living room with more money in my hand than I would have had, even if my cheques had arrived? I didn't even leave the house for goodness sake! Several of God's people had come by, knocked at the door and said, "God told me to give you this." They would hand me an envelope of cash, one for $94, another one $46 and so on, and so on. I could not believe it! Even an atheist friend gave us some cash saying, "I just felt I was supposed to do this." Weird!

This was nothing for God to pull off. But He graciously used it to teach me a mighty lesson. Our God is able to make all grace abound to you so that in all things, at all times, having all that you need, you will abound to every good work. (2 Corinthians 9:8)

He is so majestic, so brilliant. He can change a nation in a day. He can change your situations, and my situations in a moment. Nothing is too difficult for Him. Only believe.

Think of it. Think of the greatest laugh God ever had, when His enemy, satan, thought he had finally gotten rid of the Son of God by having Him crucified on an ugly cross and stuck in a hole in the ground. Satan thought: "HA! There. It's done. The story's over buddy! You lose!"

Whoops! Surrpriiiise! The stone was rolled away and Jesus came bursting forth from death in tumultuous victory! TAD-DAH! What an awesome God!

Yes, it looked well over. Jesus was completely dead. But it is never over, my friends, until God says it's over and He will have the last laugh.

And just a thought… even when we die as Christians, the story is not over; the adventure is just beginning.

For Christians, the story is NEVER over.

Going deeper…

1) So, do you like or dislike it when God acts as the 11th hour, 59th minute God? Why or why not?
2) Has God ever done that with you? Showed up at the last minute to resolve things?
3) What Biblical story do you think of when you think of God rescuing His people at the

last possible moment? Why is this story important to you?

4) What stood out for you in this chapter that might nudge you to think differently about God?

5) What does it say about the character of our God that He is never worried about time, or what the enemy is up to?

6) Is there something you can change in your thinking that will assist you in trusting Him more today?

Chapter 7
Living Life from the Inside Out

For those who are led by the Spirit of God are the sons of God. – Romans 8:14

There are four kinds of people in the world today.

Those who make things happen. Those who watch things happen. Those who wonder what just happened.

And the fourth kind of people are those who watch God make things happen and stand back in awe and wonder. I want to be in that number… the fourth category, just watching what God is doing, joining Him in that work and seeing His wonders.

When you see a sign in a restaurant window that saws Under New Management, what kind of things does that bring up in your mind? Better food? Better service? Renovations? You bet. I think every Christian should be given a sign like that when become born again. Here's your sign… Under New Management.

God's in the house and He's renovating. God is busy changing things and in fact, the old nature, the old sinful man has lost his job and there is a new Manager!

What happens when you ask Jesus to come and live in your house, your heart so to speak? We know a tiny little man does not come in and set up shop in your left ventricle. He doesn't come in a physical way. You might recall the illustrations used a great deal in the '80s of the little chair in your heart signifying the throne of your life, and Jesus sitting on it. Sometimes we push Him off the throne and then the big "I" sits up on it. That is a helpful illustration, even in its cheesiness but the question is: what really takes place in our being when we say "yes" to the Lordship of Christ in our life?

Before conversion, we are going through life bound to this earth, dead to God in our spirit, miserable in our emptiness, void of God and generally unhappy campers. Something is missing. Even if we "have it all" on this earth, without God, there's still a gap there, something missing in our life. God has created you with a God-shaped vacuum that is inside you – it really is a mystery – inside you that can only be filled by God, a place where God alone should dwell. Sometimes a demon will squat there but when God comes in, there ain't room enough for the both of them, and the demon is sent running!

After conversion, it's a different story. Something's changed. There's a spring in your step; your spirit comes alive; you're no longer bound to this earth. There's a Bible in your hand, a joy in your heart and a sparkle in your eye.

How did it happen? The scripture gives insight in 1 Thessalonians 5:23 explaining who we are as human beings created in the image of God. We are a tripartite person – we have three parts, a spirit, a soul and a body. Everybody does. We are created as spiritual beings first with a soul, in a body. Each of the three is also made up of three parts – as the psalmist said we are "fearfully and wonderfully made."

According to one long-gone theologian, the spirit consists of Communion, Conscience and Wisdom; the soul is made up of Mind, Will and Emotions, and the body of course Blood, Bone and Flesh.

Jesus comes in and dwells in us. Where? He doesn't dwell in our body or our soul. He is spirit John 4:24 says and He dwells in our spirit. It is our spirit that is eternal. We are a step above the animal world, which is why we don't see animals coming into church to find out more about Jesus. When we tell our dogs to heel, they don't stand up with their front paw out praying for someone to be touched by God. They don't have a spirit. We have a spirit; we are quite different than the animal world, despite what modern scientists are trying to sell us.

Our body – well that's obvious. There's a physical part to us that gives us our world awareness, our five senses -- our seeing, our hearing, our smell, our touch, and our taste. We are in a physical "Tent" as the apostle Paul called it. But it is not "us" in that if my arms are chopped off, I'm still me. I'm still who I am because the essence of who I am is inside.

Part of that is our soul – mind, will and emotions – which is our self-awareness. It is about what we feel, what we think, our choices or will. We are a feeling-decision-making, thinking being.

Then there's our spirit, which the Bible also calls the secret place, our innermost being where we get God-awareness and revelation. What takes place in our spirit, affects our mind, will and emotions – and our body!

We are created in the image of God, one whole being but like Him, we are three in one – spirit, soul and body. Some say we are a spirit, with a soul, in a body. And we are constantly changing both the inside and out, from glory to glory, from faith to faith and victory to victory.

On the outside, the body changes and it might become more noticeable. We stand on the scale and suck in our gut. Our spouse says, "That won't help" and we respond, "oh yes it will – now I can see the numbers on the scale… so there!"

The spirit is where God dwells. It is eternal. Before asking Christ into our life, before He comes in and quickens our spirit, we are spiritually dead and barren of that eternal life. Our spirit though is NOT inactive even though spiritually dead. In fact, they are very active spiritually, but they are not made *alive* until the Spirit of God touches them and brings them to real life, awakening them to the brightness of the glory of God in the face of Christ!

Remember that movie when the little boy says, "I see dead people" … well we all see dead people every day because their spirit is yet to have come alive in Jesus Christ. They walk around in suits and ties, and work in buildings and live in homes, but spiritually, they are dead until Christ makes them alive through faith in Him. With Christ – alive. No Christ, no life. Know Christ – Know Life!

And, when He does quicken our spirit and make us alive, He comes and dwells there in our spirit. Living life from the inside out is learning to live life by the Spirit of God, learning to keep stride with the Spirit in the midst of every day battle, learning to step back into the place of the Spirit where you can see things from God's perspective.

Jesus said that which is born of flesh is flesh and that which is born of spirit is spirit.

That is what happens every Sunday morning in churches all over the world. You basically pull your soul and body into alignment with your spirit. That is why people respond by saying, "wow, it felt so good to be in His presence."

Well, we are always in His presence, right? Where does He dwell? In your spirit! Yes, in the highest heavens but He also makes His home in our spirit by His Spirit! Incredible! When we come in His presence so to speak, we are actually stepping into that place of the spirit. We bring our mind, our will and our emotions into alignment with the Spirit of

God. Our spirit is *always* in the presence of God (once we are born again) because that is where He dwells. As a Christian, your spirit has no other focus than abiding in the presence of God; the presence of the Lord is there and we must learn to abide there too, stay there, dwell there. Rest there.

It's easier to do this at church with a bunch of believers but we need to do this every day whether we are in a secular vocation working among pre-believers, at a ministry-type job, or just in our car, at our house, at school – wherever!

As a journalist, I used to head to work in the morning thanking God for my life, my wife, my family, my job, and my car and anything else I could think of, and asking Him to use me as much as possible during the day.

I recall time after time of doing interviews when all of a sudden, the person I was interviewing would say something that would trigger my spirit and I would know that something more was happening in the kingdom realm. I would put down my pen and paper and put my pad to the side and just talk with them. Many times, there were open doors for sharing my faith in Jesus, and many opportunities to pray with people, even Members of Parliament who found themselves unloading their stuff on me despite the fact that I was a journalist! As I listened the people would pour out his or her life and we would end up praying together. They learned they could trust this journalist not to report on things that were 'off the record.'

God granted great favor with government officials, RCMP, municipal authorities and school trustees and bureaucrats at many levels. Why? Because the Lord was present and where He is, is holy.

I would pray for favor and inspiration in writing articles. I would pray "God I know that You have inspired writes before (Duh! The Bible!) so would you inspire me as I write?" And He would because I stepped back into that place of the spirit before writing. Do you think God is a good writer? Could He come up with a good lead to a story?

It became easy in a sense because I allowed Him to be in my everyday life. It has happened in stores, in coffee shops, on street corners, picking up hitch-hikers. I mean you probably relate to that feeling of being in a grocery store in the produce department when suddenly a lady begins to share with you her story and you find yourself ministering to her and thinking, "Gee, all I wanted was some bananas." But He gave you some fruit of a different kind.

And that is living from the inside out.

In the Old Testament, the Holy Spirit was poured out upon specific individuals at specific times for specific tasks but in the New Testament times He is being poured out on all flesh! And He is in you, so let Him out! Release Him!

We often pray "pour out Your Spirit, Lord," and I understand the heart in that prayer but He has been poured out. I think we need to let Him out of us because He dwells in us now and Jesus said, "Out of your innermost being will flow rivers of living water," referring to the Holy Spirit. Jesus Himself is crying, "LET ME OUT!"

It is not so much a coming down but a coming out of. I heard one speaker say that to be thirsty for God sounds spiritual but it is really quite silly because Jesus said, "If you come to me you'll never thirst again."

All you must do is learn how to get a drink, and it is from within, for Jesus dwells within by His Spirit. So, draw deeply from the well of salvation within you.

OK, how do we do that?

It begins in worship in praise, in abiding in thanksgiving. We can do that wherever we are, on our way to work or school, in the yard, at church, at the game, playing sports – literally wherever we are. We need to keep an attitude of gratitude, an attitude of worship wherever we are. Easier said than done I know, but it is possible I believe.

Think of Paul and Silas in the jail at midnight, chained up, rats running around, all damp and dark, cold and clammy. And Paul leans over to his buddy, who is barely awake and in pain, says, "Hey, you wanna sing?"

"Okay… uh, what do you want to sing?"
"I don't know how about *This is the Day*?"

They begin to praise and as they praise, things start shaking, things start rattling, chains break off as an earthquake rolls on in and BOOM the Church of Phillipi was born.

What if they hadn't? What if they just whined and complained about their trial like most people do? During a trial, God is at work and is continually trying to teach you about Himself.

What you need from Him, He wants you to teach you about.

He uses trials to break things in us, particularly the rationalistic thinking and yet God says, "don't lean unto your own understanding but trust in the Lord with all your heart and He will direct your paths."

That's so hard I know. We're always leaning unto our own understanding. But that's what gets us into trouble! I think God says step back into the place of the spirit, our secret place; step back in ME and I will direct you. See things from MY perspective.

Now, your soul is not your enemy. Your soul even desires to serve God but so often when it does, it becomes legalistically entangled doing religious stuff to work your way into a better relationship with God. It is religious gobbley-gook at its worst. It is work, work, work, doing, doing, doing instead of simply being. And, as a result you get worn out just trying to juggle everything in your life through your mind, will and emotions. It goes back to the Garden and going to the wrong tree, the tree of knowledge of good and evil rather than the Tree of Life.

Living life from the inside out is from the Spirit. There is rest there, and peace there; there is joy there. There is balance and rhythm when you have your soul living under the direction of your spirit, where God Himself calls the shots.

Your soul will rule your life TO RUIN if you let it. That's why people go up and down like a yo-yo. "I'm feeling depressed, so I'm depressed." "I don't feel like worshiping so I won't. I don't want to be a hypocrite you know."

Since when did feelings have the throne? That's why David said, "Bless the Lord O my soul!" He was bringing his soul into alignment and making it obedient. He took charge and said to his body, "Lift your hands and worship!"

Your soul processes logic but God most often if not always asks us to do things that are illogical! Think of the scriptural stories, which we have already talked about – Gideon and his great victory with a pitcher and a flame, Joshua at Jericho, David and

Goliath. Your soul does not process the illogical well – we argue and we try to figure out everything and lean on our own understanding.

But God wants you to lean on Him and His ways, His perspective, His walk of faith.

Your spirit processes revelation when God speaks. It drops into your spirit and goes deep inside beyond even the rational. Your spirit uses your soul and body for processing things but I think most Christians live in the soulish realm most of the time. Even many of our songs are soulish – which in and of itself is not bad, but it cannot define us. When you worship, you become God-conscious. You come into His rest, His fullness is there. Peace comes and you can do that – step into the place of the Spirit – anywhere, anytime, any place. The fact is you do need to position yourself in order to receive revelation from God. Expect God to speak. Ask Him to speak. Position yourself to receive from Him through your worship, adoration and praise of God.

I'll give you an example of God speaking in a way that seems impossible and what I am about to say next may seem strange to you because it was to me. I was on a prayer walk in a small community outside of Glasgow, Scotland on a beautiful night and the Lord revealed some things to me in a manner that "totally weirded me out" if you know what I mean. In fact, it was so new to me that I quenched it and shut it down, and it wasn't until I came back to Canada and thought about it some more that I realized what was really going on that night.

During this walk, I was passing by small homes on a road to my destination, a high place overlooking the village. As I went by the homes, I was praying for the people that lived there. I did not know them; I knew nothing about them. I was just praying for blessing on them. Then I felt a strong presence of the Lord and heard His voice deep inside saying, "Do you want to know how to pray for these people?"

Sure, Lord, I thought but wasn't really thinking much more than that. As I walked and prayed I began to notice things I hadn't noticed before about the yards and the homes – things like toys in the yard, or the vehicles etc. – and I started having thoughts flood my mind that I had not been thinking before, words such as, "this family is a Christian family; they love Me very much but they are in a church that is struggling…"

Up the road a way, more words: "This man is abusive to his kids…" As I listened I was praying for each home but then it began to get to me and I thought, "Wait a minute. I can't know these things! What am I doing? This is too weird!" And I shut it down.

Unfortunately, as I look back now, I realize that I started praying about other things at that moment but actually quenched His Spirit. Could it be that what was happening was that I had actually been stepping into God's perspective of things? Could He have been funneling things to me to help me pray more effectively? Perhaps it would have increased even to the place of going up to a door, knocking on it and asking to be of assistance in prayer… who knows? I don't… because I had shut the whole process down. And I have since repented of that.

Paul said, "it is not me who lives but Christ in me!" There are exciting things that can take place when we let Him out. Just release Him to be Himself in you. It is not that Christ is in us so we can copy Him, or Christ in us to help us, but in fact, it is Christ in us INSTEAD of us! It is the great exchange of my old life for His new life. He lives through us by faith. WOW!

Christ is living in me, and through me. It is an amazing mystery but what a joyful experience!

Watchman Nee said, "Say to God, I can't do this, but Your life in me can and will. The law of Christ in you will always work, always; we need to rest in it. When we realize that Christ Himself is our life and we don't need willpower, we look to Him Who is in us. The victory is His, and so therefore, ours. Christ Himself is our life, empowering and dwelling in us."

He is in us. He is for us. He is with us.

Living life from the inside out is not living a life that is impossible or forcing ourselves to be holy. When you're speaking to someone, ask Jesus what He would say if He was standing there… because He is! In you!

Everything that is demanded of you as a Christian is possible because Christ is in you. We don't need to be a superstar, we just need to be available. We don't have to be experienced before stepping out in faith believing God wants to use us. Jesus first sent out the disciples two by two when they had very little training.

I remember the story of Helen, a little old lady from Seattle who wanted to share her faith with young people so she would walk down to the University of Seattle and speak to the students there as they came and went. She had seven purses stolen during that time, so she's thinking about this. She was 74 years old but she got the idea that this could be a remarkable ministry opportunity for her! She goes out and buys all kinds of purses from thrift stores and what not, puts one thing in a purse of the day, and now lets people steal her purse! What she puts in there is a small New Testament with a note saying, "I'm very sorry that you must be so troubled that you need to steal my purse but God loves you and so do I, so if you need help, you can call me at this number."

Ya. 74 years old but she saw an opportunity, took it and makes the most of out of it. Be available. Step out.

Our soul says, "well when I have more money or when I have more time, that's when I will step out."

Our spirit, on the other hand, says, "Whatever, Father, here I am, send me."

We need to step back, live life from the inside out and see the wonders of the God Who so loves this world that He searches for people in all kinds of ways, to reach them, to touch them, to let them know His Son, Jesus lived and died for them, that they might believe on Him and have eternal life!

Sometimes people have trouble with the thought of God speaking to us apart from His written Word, but let me say again that while He does indeed speak, He will never, ever, ever, go against His written Word – EVER! He speaks in many ways so we need to unstop our ears and that well deep inside us, the well that contains His Life-Giving Spirit that Jesus referred to in John 7… "Living waters bubbling up," He said.

We do that through repentance. If there's a log jam of bitterness inside your well, blocking the flow of the Spirit of God, take it out and unstop that well of life. If there's sin inside, deal with it; take it out and get rid of it and let the water flow!

Live life from the inside out. Step back into that secret place of the Spirit, seeing things from God's perspective; join Him in His work and you'll have that sparkle in your eye, that spring in your step and people will ask you for the reason for the hope that you have.

They will literally ask you for the good news.

Going deeper…

1) What was it like when you were first born again? Describe what it felt like to be under new management.
2) How does your soul process things as opposed to your spirit?
3) Why is it important to live from the spirit as opposed to being led around by the soul?
4) What do you think of the statement most Christians live soulishly?
5) How would you describe stepping back into the place of the Spirit to be led by the Spirit, especially when things are going sideways around you?
6) What must you do for life be different in terms of making the most of every opportunity today?

Chapter 8
S'cuse me but I'm Drowning here!

Let us go over to the other side… - Mark 4:35

Did you ever notice that God always brings us into impossible situations?

I mean always is a brittle word, a strong word, but I think it fits. I did extensive study on the word 'always, and yup, it means always. He always leads us into places of whacked out impossibilities and stacked-up odds against us, and He is always amazing and always faithful.

He will ALWAYS bring you into impossible situations. Really? Why? Because He wants you to learn to trust Him and Him alone to be all you ever need.

Think of Moses having been a shepherd for 40 years in the middle of nowhere, having God speak to him and say, "Go deliver my people, Mo… and here, here is a stick." Impossible against the might of Pharaoh! But not for ALMIGHTY God! It seemed that Moses spent the first 40 years of his life thinking he was *the man* and that he could accomplish great things even for God, his own way mind you – killing an Egyptian man. But then he spent the next 40 years of his life learning that he really is not *the man* but that he really is nothing. Then God use the last 40 years of his life to show

how He can use a nothing and make something totally spectacular happen. God loves humility.

How about Shadrach, Meshach and Abednego? Talk about an impossible situation! I mean they were actually thrown in the fire! But once again, God comes through.

Think of David running out against a guy nine feet tall who was wearing a headdress that made him appear another three or four feet taller – and he was threatening the youngster, telling him he was going to feed him to the birds! Impossible situation.

Think of Paul and over 200 guys shipwrecked, some who didn't even know how to swim. Think about those guys in the water spouting away. All of them are saved from drowning because they heed the Word of God in the middle of an impossible situation.

Then there's the disciples in the boat screaming at Jesus, "LORD DON'T YOU EVEN CARE IF WE DROWN??!!"

So often, He is the 11th hour, 59th minute God, waiting until the last possible moment to come rescue us. But He's never late. He's always on time. His time.

And, even if he doesn't rescue us, said the three Hebrew teens about to be thrown into the King's fiery furnace, "we will still serve Him and not worship your idols."

That's what they said! Even if our God does not save us, we will worship only Him.

The youth at our church are fond of saying, "if they beat us up, God will heal us. If they kill us, we'll be with God, so get pumped up!

There is so much in that story in Mark 4 where Jesus is in the boat, asleep in the stern in the middle of a raging storm.

You see He had clearly said to the disciples, "Let's go over to the other side." I'm not even sure He knew there was going to be a storm coming their way, but He only did what the Father told Him, so when the Father says, "let's go to the other side" then they are going over to the other side, storm or no storm. That's why He could sleep.

I was on the Sea of Galilee recently and asked the boat captain about the squalls that were said to come up so quickly.
"Are they really like that here?" I asked.

Captain David Carmel said, "absolutely! I literally lost my main mast just last week because of a quick storm."

Ok, so this was no fairy tale. These storms on the Galilee can be extremely rough.

First, I would say that Jesus is always saying to us, "Let's go over." It might be to the other side, or here or there, but He is always on the move in our life. And He's not going "under," He's going over! He leads us from a place of victory, not defeat. There is always movement and mobility, motion and flexibility. He is continually shaping us into the word that He has spoken over us – oh my goodness, that's could be a whole 'nother chapter! He speaks words over us prophetically – to our spirit inside, or through somebody encouraging us, words of destiny and anointing, which totally launches things in us – and then He shapes us into the very word He has spoken over us. And, that my friends, is going *over to the other side.* We grow. We gain faith… and it's a journey.

The scriptures record that, "leaving the crowd behind, they took Him along, just as He was, in the boat" (Mark 4:36).

Right off the bat we see that in following Jesus, there is a leaving behind that takes place. You must leave the crowd behind when you follow Him. Did you ever notice that the closer Jesus go to the day of crucifixion, the more He seemed to make it harder for people to follow Him? He increasingly said things that would cause offense (on purpose!) and controversy, such as "he who does not hate his father and mother is not worthy to be called my disciples," and "You have to count the cost in following me," "eat my flesh and drink my blood. "Deny yourself, take up your cross (die) daily," and much, much more. It is not an easy thing to follow Christ; it goes against the grain of society, against the natural – because it is a supernatural thing, even to follow Him. There is a real leaving that takes place.

The Bible says that in marriage there is a leaving as well, a cleaving and a weaving that occurs. "For this reason, a man shall leave his father and mother, cleave unto his own wife, and the two shall become one flesh" (Genesis 2:24). It is unhealthy for a married couple to *not* leave a father and mother, continually clinging on to the old way of life, the old way of doing things. And just like that, in our relationship with Christ, there is also a leaving that takes place, a cleaving unto Him, and in fact, it is His desire that we become one with Him (so there's a weaving too).

Secondly the story goes on to say that they took Him along just as He was. I never noticed the phrase "Just as He was" until more recently. What does that mean? So often, I think we have a distorted view of Jesus. For some He is the meek, mild, weakling Jesus that is depicted in some artists' renditions as effeminate and limp-wristed, with product in His hair, which is blowing in the wind like Fabio's. For others, He is seen more like the distant president or direction of operations in the universe. They'd recognize Him maybe if they saw Him but there's no relationship. For others He is the Lion, the angry Jesus who flips tables and makes whips to confront sinners. In their minds, He is just waiting to pounce on you as soon as you make a mistake.

But those disciples took Jesus into their boat "just as He was." We must take Him into our boat just as He is. He is both the Lion and the Lamb. He is gentle, yes but He is also the consuming fire, both meek and mighty, innocent and jealous, kind, righteous, lowly, humble and bold with eyes blazing like fire! We must take Him as he is, not our distorted Jesus, the one who doesn't confront, or on the other hand, the one who does not love. He is the expression of the Father, all of Him. Are you ready for that?

So back to the boat. You know there were at least four well trained fishermen in that boat that day, and all of them are terrified, fighting for their lives because the waves were buffeting the boat with a fury. The sea was angry that day... You almost have to wonder if this storm was produced supernaturally by the enemy to destroy them. Finally, one of them gets up enough courage to wake the Master up, probably Peter wouldn't you say? And Peter asks Him if He cares that they drown. I don't think it was a calm question, a quiet, polite Canadian question. I think it was a bang-your-first-on-the-dashboard-of-life-kind-of-burst-out-loud rant like HELLO! DON'T YOU CARE IF WE DROWN HERE???!!!

Ever been there? Ever feel like you're about to lose it? Ever lose it? Ever cry out, "Jesus! Don't You even care?! Do you see me down here? Do you hear me?"

And then in His time, He answers you in some way that you didn't expect and you sheepishly (good word) say, "oops, sorry Lord."

Those disciples were fully enrolled in the real Jesus School, weren't they? And, at this point they were actually failing, which gives us all hope I'd say.

When Jesus stood up, wiped His eyes and commanded the winds and waves to "Be Still!" a lesson was about to be given. Yep, here it comes.

They looked around them. Right in front of their eyes, the waves rocked their way to an even flatness of glass; the winds simply died down and the squall is totally gone. As they were sitting there wiping water from their faces, I can hear them saying… "omg." OH. MY. GOD.

And can you see Jesus turning and smiling and saying, "Exactly boys!"

He asks them two questions, two deep penetrating questions, which is very common for Him. He asks, "Why were you so afraid?"

"What?? S'cuse me, but we were drowning like right here in the boat!"
Another may have cried out, "C'mon Jesus, we were going to die! I can still taste the water in my

mouth; we're drenched here! Look, look there's a fish in my pocket!"

But the key word in that question is the smallest one of the bunch – the word, "so" – why were you *so* afraid? Fear is not always a bad thing. Fear is like the indicator light on your dashboard flashing, "hello up there, time to do something!" But the Lord always says, "Do not fear." In the original Hebrew scriptures, it would have read do not DO fear.

Fear comes and fear causes a reaction. Our reaction in the boat in the middle of a storm should be to rise in the face of fear, full of faith in the One who saves. Most of the time though if you're like me, the first reaction is a far cry from the calm, confident, peaceful response. It is more like the disciples' wail of "Don't you care??!!"
When fear flashes up, what we do with it is the key – we are to go to God in faith, trusting in His Word. Do not PANIC!

The second question He asks is, "Where is your faith?" It's like Jesus was saying "Don't you get it? Don't you know who I am? Don't you know Who you have in your boat? I *only* do what I see the Father doing, and upon His word I move. I am with you. I said we were going to the other side so we are going to the other side. Trust me. Faith, guys, it's all about faith. Without faith, you can't even please the Father at all."

The fact of the matter is that right in the middle of our raging storm, when everything else is screaming out in opposition, He simply wants us to get it. Get it? Trust Him! He is with you in your boat!

So, the sea has calmed down. Life is good. Immediately, says the scripture, immediately they came to the other side. Must have been a Holy Ghost outboard motor, or the angels stepped in and whisked them to the other side. Wow. Imagine now the guys laughing and whooping it up, elbowing each other.
"I wasn't afraid; you were so afraid!"
"Shaddup! I was totally fine. It was James and John doing all the yellin'." Ah, boys will be boys, eh?

Laughter and joyful jostling. The boat eases into the beach with the familiar crunching wood-on-sand-and-rock sound and the laughter is suddenly 'drowned' out with another new, louder sound.

A man, a stark-naked man that is, comes running out of the bushes onto the beach, screaming at the top of his lungs, arms flailing around. Did I mention that he's naked? He's totally demonized screaming, "AAAAHHHHHAHHRRRG" What are you doing here? What do you want with me, Jesus, Son of the Most High God? Swear to God You won't torture me!!" He is screeching and screaming at the top of his voice.

I can hear the deafening silence of the disciples now as they are thinking: "Right. Okay. I think I'll just say here in my comfortable little boat, thanks. That's alright. You go Jesus. I'll stay here. Thank you very much."

Can you see the ways of God? Can you see that one victorious moment, one lesson from Jesus, often leads us right smack dab into the sheer impossibility of the next one? That's how we grow; that's how we increase in our faith, one step at a time, daily into new things. From glory to glory He is changing us. That's an awful wonderful thought if you get my drift, a very scary, exciting time.

Jesus totally sets this demonized man free. Here he is hanging out at the tombs, chained and bound, out of his mind and Jesus comes along and sets him free. It's kind of a picture of the church, sometimes isn't it?

Hanging around death and dead things, dead religion, dead traditions, bound and chained to man's ways, not free at all, not even in our right minds so to speak. Then Jesus comes and set us free.

The next scene shows the man, sitting with Jesus, in his right mind, newest of clothes and totally free. He ends up going home and spreading the good news, which is also what the church is supposed to be doing. Another impossible situation taken care of by the precious and magnificent Son of God.

I heard someone say once that the miracle wasn't so much in the calming of the storm outside as it was in the calming of the man inside.

At any moment, Jesus can calm the storm around you, silence it with just a word, but more importantly, He wants to calm the storm within you, help you learn how to trust in Him right in the middle of the impossibilities surrounding your life.

If you look through the driving rain, if you strain to see through the winds, wiping the rain and water from your eyes, you'll see Him. Yup, there He is. He is striding across the deck of your ship so to speak; He's walking right toward you and He has a smile on His face that says everything's going to be alright. It's a joyful and all-confident smile. He has something tucked under His arm that you can't quite make out. As He gets closer, He laughs as the boat rocks His step a little. He's not worried, not at all. Nothing takes Him by surprise. He's your hero. He's your champion and He's coming right to you! As He reaches you, He deftly swings out what is under His arm. It's a blanket – a picnic blanket! He throws it out in front of you and you quickly remember, "He sets a table before me in the presence of my enemies" (Psalm 23:5) and you realize that indeed, everything is going to be okay.

I'm reminded of one the most memorable moments in recent Olympic history. It took place in 1992 at the Summer Olympic Games in Barcelona, Spain. A British runner named Derek Redman had been through 22 surgeries after an injury he suffered while getting ready for the 400-meter race in the 1988 Olympics in Seoul, Korea. Yet there he was competing again.

People were amazed that he was running again, let alone being in the Olympics representing Great Britain. The gun goes off. The runners bolted. He was in the middle of the pack of some of the fastest runners on the planet when, about halfway around the track, he pulled his hamstring and wiped out.

Of course, everyone thought he was done; the broadcasters started yelling, "Derek Redman is out of the race! Derek Redman is out of the race!" The cameraman stayed with the rest of the runners as they finished the race but then raced back to Derek Redman who was still down on the track, trying to pull himself back up. He was determined to finish the race!

It seemed that the crowd simply forgot about the winner and turned to watch this great athlete slowly stand up and start to hobble around the track in intense pain. You can see this on the video footage. As you watch his face, there were tears streaming down his cheeks. Yet despite his determination, it was obvious there was just no way he was going to finish; he was in way too much pain.

The crowd continue to watch in silent amazement, then some cheering, some with hands clamped over their mouths as Redman was about to collapse again. Just then a man came running down out of the stands. He climbed the fence at the side of the track, got by the security guards and ran out onto the track. It was his father!

He had been sitting in a section at the top of the grand stands that day; he could not imagine anything except getting involved.

For years, he had been there by his son's side, getting up at 4 a.m. for practices, encouraging, supporting and cheering his son on. Now, he felt he just could not stand by and let his son fail to finish the race.

So, he came jogging up to his injured boy, and when he got close enough, he reached for him, putting his hand on Derek's shoulder. The young man took a few more painful steps and then turned and fell into the chest of his mentor dad. Then Jim Redman said these words, which were later quoted by almost every newspaper covering the Games. He said, "Derek, we started this thing together and we are going to finish this thing together."

Then Jim took his son's arm, put it around his own shoulders, put his arm around Derek's shoulders and held his son up. I mean, literally just held him up as together they made their way around the rest of the track. As you can imagine, the crowd was now roaring its approval as Derek Redman finished his race, supported by his father.

No, he did not finish it alone. Together, linked arm in arm, Father and Son crossed the finish line as one. The crowd cheered. Who won? Don't know. Derek Redman finished the race with his father by his side. That's what I remember.

Our Father runs with us. He cheers us on with the great crowd of witness (Hebrews 12:1) letting us know we can trust Him totally. Lean on Him. Oh, there will be opposition, and there will be falls, challenges and disappointments (probably more like a marathon than a sprint, or a steeplechase than an oval track) but with Him by our side, lifting us up, we can make it. We can get to the other side!

So, eyes off the storm. Eyes on Jesus. Run your race!

Going deeper...

1) Do you agree with the statement that God *always* brings us into impossible situations? Why or why not?
2) What do you think it means that God is always on the move in our life, and always going over to the other side?
3) What does it mean for God to be changing us from glory to glory? What is happening between each glory?
4) Describe what it means to have a leaving, a cleaving and a weaving in our relationship with Jesus Christ.

5) Why would God bring us into impossible situations?
6) What is God trying to form in us when everything looks bleak and impossible?

Chapter 9
The Questioning God

What are you doing here, Elijah? - 1 Kings 19:9

So, why would the God of the universe, the King of Kings and Lord of Lords, He who rules supremely in all matters everywhere, any time, any place, ask a puny human being a question?

I mean think about it. He doesn't really need any answers, does He? No. The thing is, He doesn't ask questions to get information. So then, what's the big idea?

When God asks us a question, He's simply helping us get to where we need to get to, because it is not where we're at physically, it is where we are at spiritually that matters. Right?

The first we see of it is actually in the creation story where God is walking in the garden in the cool of the day and the Lord called out to the man, "Adam, where are you?" (Genesis 3:9) and Adam is hiding from God.

God knew exactly where Adam was hiding, and Eve for that matter too, but the truth is: they didn't. They were ashamed. They were hiding. They needed to come out of hiding and declare themselves. They needed to come before the Lord and humbly admit that they had disobeyed. God knew that, and so He asks, "Adam, where are you?"

Later in Genesis 32:27, we find that God comes down as a man (probably a pre-incarnate Jesus Christ actually) and wrestles with Jacob at one point, asking ol' Jake, "what is your name?"

Now why would God need to ask Jacob, the grandson of God's good friend, Abraham, what his name is? Again, He knows it already! So why is He asking the question? Ponder that thought.

The answer is found in the meaning of Jacob's name – schemer, deceiver, trickster. Jacob needed to declare himself before God.

Jacob needed to humble himself, bow low and admit, "my name is Schemer. I am a liar, a deceiver."

And it is at that point when Jacob comes out of hiding so to speak, that God declares a new identity over him.

"You shall no longer be called Jacob, but Israel because you have struggled with God and man and have overcome..." (Genesis 32:28). Israel on the other hand, means "prince of God, or he will rule (as God) and overcomer" but again Jacob needed to declare where he was at before God changed him from the inside out. Can you imagine what it would have been like to be called a schemer all your life, then in one moment your whole life changes because you are now an overcomer? If you have ever experienced the true touch of Jesus in your life, you can no doubt relate to Jacob. And it is interesting to see that the man formerly known as Jacob… leaves the scene with a permanent limp from the touch of God. Just a little reminder of the power of God and the weakness of man.

Think of Elijah on the mountain in 1 Kings 18 challenging and wiping out the prophets of Baal and his mistress, gaining a massive victory over the religious spirit of the day, and then later even outrunning a horse-driven chariot down through the Jezreel Valley. But in only a matter of hours, he ends up running for his life and hiding in a desert cave, afraid of a wicked queen named Jezebel, who wants to lop off his head.

Despite a huge victory that God had obtained for him in front of everybody, Elijah now wanders off into a month of aimlessness, winding up in a cave on Mt. Horeb where God shows up big time… and asks him a simple question.

"What are you doing here, Elijah?" Once again, God is giving opportunity for the man to speak his heart, whine about being the "only one left" who follows God, about feeling lonely and abandoned, about all the stuff inside that had been bottled up for that season. And God meets him right there and deals with his stuff before sending him on his way in a better place.

All through scripture, God comes and asks these simple yet penetrating questions.

He asks Jeremiah, "What do you see?"

In the New Testament, you see Jesus asking questions like, "Where is your husband?" to the woman at the well whom He knows has had five husbands and is currently shacking up with a different dude. He asks a beggar, "do you want to be made whole?" Well ya! Isn't it obvious? Apparently not.
Apparently, God needs to prompt us to declare where we are at, and what we really desire deep down before He promotes us into the next step of the journey. I mean, he asks a bind man, "what do you want from me?"

In asking a blind man that, He is asking more than whether the man wants to see. He is asking whether the guy wants to give up his whole identity as a blind beggar. He is asking if he is willing to now go out and work for an honest day's wage, whether he is willing to return to his family, and be restored into society. Everything changes when Jesus stops by and asks you a question! So, He asks these questions to see if we realize that.

He asks the disciples, "what do you want me to do for you?" He asks a crowd of hundreds who are drinking like crazy at the Feast of Tabernacles, "is anyone thirsty?"

He asks His friends, "who do you say that I am?"
He asks Peter, "do you love me?"

So, my question for you is: what is He asking you these days?

"Where are you?"
"What is your name?"
"What are you doing here?"
"What do you see?"
"What do you want me to do for you?"
"Are you thirsty?"
"Who do you say that I am?"
"Do you love me?"

He asks these kinds of questions not because He doesn't know the answer but because He loves you and wants you to declare it. He wants you to humbly come before Him and tell Him your heart and where you're at, because He knows that when you're brutally honest before Him, and honest with yourself, you're actually doing yourself a great big favor.

And He waits for you. Did you know that?

In Isaiah 30:18, we see that God is sitting and waiting for you and me to approach Him. In the Amplified Version it reads like this: "Therefore the Lord (earnestly) waits – expectant, looking and longing – to be gracious to you, and therefore he lifts Himself up that He may have mercy on you and show lovingkindness to you; for the Lord is a God of Justice. Blessed – happy, fortunate (to be envied) are all those who (earnestly) wait for Him, who expect and look and long for Him (for His victory, His favor, His love, His peace, His joy and His matchless, unbroken companionship.)"

WOW! Read that again, slowly.

What is God waiting for? We always think we are waiting for Him to act and yet He is waiting for us! He waits for us to come to Him, to declare ourselves, to declare where we are at, to confess our sin, to give Him everything, to allow Him to change our name, our identity, from sinner to saint, from deceiver to overcomer! He is waiting for us to come to Him because He longs to have compassion on us!

So, another question I have for you is "why wait any longer?"

Just put the book down, kneel if you can, but take time right now where you are, even if it's in a busy coffee shop, and breathe a prayer to the Lord Jesus Christ telling Him that you are thirsty for Him, that you want Him to take over the control of your life. Declare that He is Lord, and that you're sorry for trying to run the show. Give it up. Give it all to Him and let Him lead you into the exciting life of hearing His voice every day, following Him in every way, and bearing eternal fruit that honors His name.

It's time to be one of those polished arrows in His quiver that He takes out and uses for war! It's time to add the super to your natural and let Him live through you like never before. It's time to be a fully devoted follower of Jesus Christ! It's time to start living life from the inside out!

Going deeper…

1) Has God ever asked you a question? Describe a time when He prompted a question in your life.
2) What was His objective in asking you the question?
3) What do you think He was getting at in asking Jacob his name?
4) Was there any Biblical character you related to more than another in this chapter?
5) How important is it to know our identity in Christ? To know our new name in Him?
6) Read Ephesians 1 and count how many times the phrase "in Christ" or "in Him" is used. What does this say about who we are?

Chapter 10
Transition is Forever!

And we, who with unveiled faces, all reflect the
Lord's glory, are being transformed into His
likeness with ever-increasing glory, which comes
from the Lord, who is Spirit – 2 Corinthians 3:18

Every time I turn around and ask someone how they
are doing lately, it seems like they are saying, "well,
I'm in transition, you know?"

I've realized now that no matter what anybody says,
transition is forever, my friend.

We are always changing, or else we die. That's it.
Change or die. Medically speaking, that's true; we
change or we die. Stop changing and it's over. We
are forever growing and dying, dying and growing,
both physically and spiritually.

We who are following Christ, are always changing,
from glory to glory the scriptures say, from faith to
faith and from victory to victory. God wants us to
change, expects us to change and enables and
empowers us to change. He speaks words over our
lives, then takes the time to shape us into the words
He has spoken over us. It is His work. We are His
workmanship (Ephesians 2:10), His craftsmanship
and He shapes us into vessels of honor to be used
for His purposes for the praise of His glory
(Ephesians 1:14). But if we resist changing, we will

end up back in the ol' water bucket or slapped back down on the potter's wheel. Ouch. Let me explain.

In Isaiah 49:2, God uses a phrase to describe His servant Isaiah as that of "a polished arrow" hidden in His quiver. I think that we can appropriate that picture to our lives. Do you know how they made arrows back then? It was quite a process.

Take a deep breath and read this in one breath: Yes, quite a process of finding the right kind of branch or stick, dropping it into a bucket of water for a time of soaking (until it was so waterlogged that it sunk to the bottom of the bucket), then taking it out and stretching it on a rack into a straight line, letting it dry there in the hot sun, whittling to a point on one end, sticking in some tail feathers on the other, and then adjusting those feathers to make it fly right so that it can hit the target when need be. Then polish it. Whew!

That is the picture of the Christian life. We are found by God under a rock somewhere, buried and bent up under the garbage and crap of the world. He grabs hold of us tightly in His hand and we are taken back to His house along with many other 'sticks'. We are then dropped into the water bucket of church life and we begin to soak and soak and soak, until we get kind of waterlogged. We sink. It seems we aren't really useful to anybody; we just lie there on the bottom of the bucket watching life go by.

I heard one evangelist taking about this time in his life as being a bottom dweller in the sea of humanity. He had gotten saved was immediately a 'shark' he said, going about trying to attack everybody with the Gospel's good news. He even left tracts tucked into the toilet paper rolls he encountered so it would drop out when unrolled. The fruit of his labors didn't amount to much – and as a result he became a bottom dweller, a guppy so to speak and just watched life go by. Then he came through a process based on the parable of the sower, realizing that his responsibility was simply to sow the seed in joy – like a dolphin! With a smile on his face, he just went about sowing seed and enjoying the good things of the kingdom. Fruit followed as he left the growing to the Grower and the sowing to the sower. From shark, to guppy to dolphin – a good picture of many Christian lives.

Now, back to the water bucket. After some time, the Master Archer rescues us once again out of the doldrums of bucket-dwelling and stretches us into upright, mature living.

He then brings into focus or sharpens out the point of our life – which by the way can be painful as He whittles away the bits and pieces that are not Christlike – and He give us some guidance feathers in the form of mentors, fathers and mothers in the faith who help us fly straight. He takes us out and aims us at a target. If we miss the target on that particular outing… well it might mean going back to the water bucket! We don't fail. We just get to learn again. This is a life-long journey. But it is only after we hit the target a few times, and a good deal of polishing… that He tucks us away in His quiver for that special season. This arrow is meant for war!

Then there's the potter's wheel. Remember Jeremiah 18? God instructs Jeremiah to go down to the potter's house and listen there to a message that the Lord would give him. So, he goes down and sees that "the pot he was shaping from the clay was marred in his hands, so the potter formed it into another pot, shaping as seemed best to him. (Jeremiah 18:4).

The Lord is the Master Potter and is shaping us all the time. Indeed, we are marred in His hands. The original meaning of that word is 'ruined.' Well, it is a good place to be ruined – in the hands of the Master Potter. But know in the depths of your being that He is One shaping us; He is the One molding us and He is the One Who is making us into a useful vessel of honor.

The scriptures say the Potter is shaping the vessel into what seems best to Him. It is so good to know that the Lord knows what He has in mind as He shapes us. We are marred in His hands. We have sinned, all of us, and fallen short of His standards and missed the mark or the target of His glory. And, as He shapes us, He makes us, conforms and forms us into what He wants us to be.

Even when Jesus said, "Follow me and I will *make* you fishers of men," the Greek word for 'make' literally means to form, construct and shape. It's what He does. He shapes us. It is His work. Sometimes it no doubt means that He splats us down on the wheel when we seem to be resisting His good hand of mercy in our lives.

That story in Jeremiah show us that God has in mind a vision for our lives that He is forming. The key is to submit to the process and trust Him to do what is best and right.

Another way to look at this is taken from the ever-familiar Psalm 23. This psalm is read out at so many funerals, seen in Hollywood movies so many times that we get numb to it. But the shepherd writes in Psalm 23 that the Lord *makes me* lie down in green pastures.

The word "make" there is a commanding word which literally means to put or hold down. Think of it. It is a strong word. Sometimes God will *make us* lay down. You see what I mean?

Shepherds will tell of how they sometimes have to go as far as breaking the leg of a sheep that keeps wandering off, putting itself and other sheep in danger. By breaking the leg, the sheep must trust the shepherd who then feeds it by hand and nurses it back to health. It is for its own good. God too is soooo into shaping our character into what He desires us to be, that He will even allow hard things to come into our life in order to shape us into that vessel of honor He has in mind.

Think of Job, or Moses, or David, or Jesus even, who was ejected *by the Spirit* into the desert for a time of testing and being tempted by the devil. The book of Hebrews says Jesus learned obedience by suffering – should we expect anything less in our own case?

Our character is so important because it is the vessel that holds the anointing and destiny of our lives. Sometimes we think or pray, "Oh God give me my destiny! NOW!" But if He did, without having shaped our character into proper place, we could not sustain or bear up under the weight of the destiny He has for us. We'd wipe out. And, then reproach is brought upon the name of Christ because of our poor witness in our lives, hypocrisy and whatnot. And then God would have to send us back to the water bucket, or back onto the wheel of His merciful judgment.

So, we see that the shaping of our character is indeed forever. Change is forever. Transition is forever. He is sanctifying (big word for shaping us) through and through, according to 1 Thessalonians 5:23 in our spirit, soul and body, keeping us "blameless" until the coming of our Lord Jesus Christ. It is a life-long process.

So, I say, hang on folks. It is a ride of a lifetime, full of many short cuts and long cuts, adventures, mountains and valleys, times of great trial, wind and waves and times of amazing green and peaceful pastures.

The key is in the submission as I said, the coming under the protection of (that's what submission really means) to God and His ways, His heavenly protocol and His wisdom. He obviously allows in His wisdom what He could have stopped in His power – but is always unto or up to something. He is always training, always shaping, always molding, constructing us into the image of His Son whom He loves.

We often hear Christians quoting Romans 8:28 about all things working *for good* for those who are called according to His purpose… but you don't often hear the next verse being quoted along with it – to be *conformed to the image of His Son.* That is the "good" He is talking about.

So, don't resist His love, His discipline, His shaping. Submit to Him; submit to the process of being made into a glorious vessel of honor through which He can pour out all the goodness of His kingdom to the people around you. He wants to pour out healing oil, fine new wine; He wants to display the splendor of His fruit in you.

So, the bottom line is to stay the course, set your face like flint against the wind and carry on. You don't know how far you've come, and you don't know what is just around the corner.

Do everything He asks you to do, even the outrageous, illogical things that go against all human reasoning.

Kiss the Bear!

Going deeper...

1) Have you experienced life in the water bucket? What was it like to be soaking in the new Christian life, only to find yourself suddenly at the bottom of the bucket?
2) Have you felt put on a shelf in some way as a vessel being shaped and then left to dry?
3) Has there ever been a time when you felt like you were in a kiln being fired, perhaps with others at the same time, where you almost gave it all up?
4) Have you ever experienced hitting the target? Or being used by God to pour fresh healing oil out on someone? Or new wine for someone? What was that like?
5) Why is it important to know that the process of sanctification is life long?
6) Define sanctification in your own words.
7) Why is it important to remember Romans 8:29 along with Romans 8:28?
8) Submission is not a good word in our society today. Why is it still a good, relative

and pertinent word in the scriptures for us today?

9) After reading this book, what do you think it means now to Kiss the Bear?

Made in the USA
Columbia, SC
01 October 2018